EATING THE INTERNET

EATING THE INTERNET

CONSUMING DIGITAL FOOD MEDIA

ANABELLE NUELLE

NEW DEGREE PRESS

EATING THE INTERNET

Consuming Digital Food Media

ISBN   978-1-64137-167-4   *Paperback*

        978-1-64137-168-1   *Ebook*

To the internet, and kitchens everywhere.

CONTENTS

INTRODUCTION   WHY I WROTE THIS   9

PART 1.   **A KID WITH AN ANDROID AND A**
                   TREACHEROUS SPACE   **15**
CHAPTER 1.   CROISSANTS, COMPUTERS, AND
                  COMMUTERS   19
CHAPTER 2.   UNCERTAIN TERRAIN   29

PART 2.   **ACCESS**   **41**
CHAPTER 3.   EVERYONE'S A FOODIE   47
CHAPTER 4.   NEW CHANNELS   61
CHAPTER 5.   NEW VOICES AND FLAVORS   69

PART 3.   **CONNECT**   **81**
CHAPTER 6.   MAKING IT PERSONAL   85
CHAPTER 7.   "INSTAGRAM, A COMMUNITY OF
                  OVER 1 BILLION..."   97
CHAPTER 8.   CONNECTION OFFLINE   107

PART 4.   **ENGAGE**   **121**

CHAPTER 9.   THE OLD IS NEW AGAIN   123

CHAPTER 10.   THE TRUST TEST   135

CHAPTER 11.   THE ENGAGEMENT EMPIRE   145

                ACKNOWLEDGMENTS   161

                APPENDIX   163

INTRODUCTION

WHY I WROTE THIS

___

In February of 2018, I sat in the heated porch of a coffee shop in Georgetown, DC. A need for coffee and quiet solitude had forced me from my apartment; spotty cell service had sent me to the semi-insulated porch despite the sharp chill of that grey morning. I took a call with the simple intention to gather information, needing only a quick thirty minutes to poke around a subject and measure my interest. An hour later, I had filled six full pages of my notebook with frantic scribbling, arrows pushing ideas from page to page around which my handwriting bent and twisted to fit as many words as my half frozen fingers could manage.

Information gathering had turned conversational, half way between a curious questioning and collaborative brainstorm. Data collection evolved into interview, the first of many I would conduct for this book. At the click of the call's end, I flipped back through my notes—I circled ideas related to culture, underlined comments about technology, outlined quotes regarding people's relationship to each other and the world, bolded over mentions of change and re-drew the arrows connecting them all. Before me, almost every topic unfolded: politics, art, entertainment, technological development, psychology, business, community, and connecting it all—food and its manifestations online.

I scheduled the call because I was interested in the ceaseless appearances of one minute or less recipe videos on my and my peers' newsfeeds. They were everywhere, and if they weren't there, an Eater or Thrillist listicle, an article from *Bon Appetit* or *The New York Times*, or a cooking show from *Tastemade* was. I was interested in how something so layered in culture, everyday habit, and sensory experience found a place in the two dimensions of the digital world. I was intrigued by the methods of publishers, brands and media outlets for handling this content on ever-morphing platforms. I couldn't understand how cooking and dining could be captured fairly in the buzz of social media. Rather, I was convinced it couldn't be and braced myself to hear more evidence for a case against social media and furthered by technology's inauthenticity.

But, I was wrong.

Yes, the people, brands and industries creating content,building a loyal following in the unpredictable digital terrain, were frustrated—there exists no cemented guidebook on how to capture food content and navigate the many digital platforms. No, there is no digital equal to the satisfaction of biting into a fresh burger, hot off the grill or sitting around a table to enjoy a traditional family dinner. But where I expected impossible obstacles and a cheapening of the subject matter, I found new opportunities and an unexpected richness in today's relationship between food and food media.

In this book, you'll find my exploration of the frustrations, the shortcomings, the obstacles, the new opportunities and the emerging vibrancy of new media. Equipped with the research I've done and motivated by the conversations I've had, I wrote this book to define and defend what I refer to as the 'food internet'—the summation of any and all food media online.

I cover Instagram, *Yelp*, the *New York Times*, new apps and more. The breadth and enormity of the food internet prevents me from covering every actor in this sphere while its ceaseless development promises some information included will be outdated by the weeks between writing and publishing— the static of printed word. Accordingly, this book tries to do no more than survey, filtering down examples to best emphasize patterns I see motivating the food internet as a whole.

I open the book by setting the scene of the digital realm, nodding to the challenges of the food internet and its offline impact, and break the book into three themed sections in accordance to the aforementioned patterns visible in contemporary food media:

- Access—the open nature of this content and its digital manifestations
- Connection—the desire to connect with people and communities
- Engagement—the action motivated by this content, frequently taken offline

In my digital subject matter, I found a wealth of humanity and a complimentary nature in digital media to real, offline food experiences.

For readers working on the creation side of the food internet, I hope the themes and examples I provide give order to this ever-shifting sphere. I do not pretend to know what technology will come next and do not venture into specific trends, but instead, I try to offer guidelines motivating its change and consumer interaction. For readers on the consumer side, I hope this book lends new perspective to food media, sparking an appreciation for it as slightly more than menial entertainment.

Most of all, I hope you finish this book seeing clearly the connection between offline and online life, aware of how one reinforces the other but lands always in offline experience.

Thank you, and enjoy.

PART I:

A KID WITH AN ANDROID AND A TREACHEROUS SPACE

"In the next few years, the scrawny kid hunched over his Android may become as important to the success of a restaurant as the chef.

While nobody was paying attention, food quietly assumed the place in youth culture that used to be occupied by rock 'n' roll—individual, fierce and intensely political, communal yet congenial to aesthetic extremes."

—*JONATHAN GOLD, LOS ANGELES TIMES*[1]

By the time of this publication, that quote will be about a decade old and its veracity all the more obvious. In the span of that decade, a great many things have changed in our tangible and digital lives, namely, our tangible and digital lives have been permanently intermixed. Their inextricable union adjusted when we get our news, how we communicate with friends, how we find information, what tools we use to find our way around, and where we spend our money. Most importantly for Gold and the purposes of this book, the intermingling of off and online worlds changed the way we eat, what we eat, and how we interact with food.

---

1   Gold, Jonathan. 2009. "A Year In Food: Changing Tastes". *Los Angeles Times*, , 2009. http://articles.latimes.com/2009/dec/27/opinion/la-oe-gold27-2009dec27.

Instagram, Snapchat, Facebook, *Yelp* shuffled food, its makers, and its infinite shapes into the public and viral eye. Thousands shared monstrous shakes, enjoying together a sense of a bewilderment at videos starring milk shakes whose candy coated sides miraculous chocolates, cookies and pretzels floating in a delirium of whipped cream, a sugar coma inducing cloud on which an entire piece of chocolate cake rests. Home cooks found a new calling, growing the blogging population with personal narrative and practical recipes, framed by pleasing photography of freshly baked goodies. The average teenager, now young adult, found a fresh joy and status in standing on a chair to snap a picture of brunch while dining companions wait with the irritated growl of an empty stomach. The size of food publishers' digital and print teams flipped to give digital the upper hand and the adjective 'viral' lost its connotation with illness. Star restaurant owners and chefs shared the blue-glow of the digital spotlight with their plated creations and crafted experiences, while the larger industry added another box to tick: "please the internet."

What and how to do this remains an unanswerable question. Even Ed Levine, the founder of *Serious Eats*, admitted in a recent podcast episode, that "if [he] wanted to launch *Serious Eats* right now … The climate has changed so dramatically in digital media that nobody would give me money now, even though *Serious Eats* is seen as this great website with

10 million unique visitors a month."[2] Content creators over populate the space, consumer attention divides into niche communities around singular small celebrities, publishers, brands, advertisers and up and individuals compete for the attention of the everyday user and with a single change a platform can override a space.

Welcome to the Food Internet, a colorful, ever changing community and consequently an unnerving new space.

2   Serious Eats. 2018. "Phil Rosenthal Is Anthony Bourdain Except Afraid Of Everything". Podcast. *Serious Eats*. https://www.seriouseats.com/2018/02/special-sauce-phil-rosenthal-is-anthony-bourdain-except-afraid-of-everything.html.

CHAPTER 1

CROISSANTS, COMPUTERS, AND COMMUTERS

———

A fifty-minute train ride along Chicago's North Shore will bring you to the Winnetka village train station and the essence of French baking. Tucked into the small brick train station is a single service window that opens up to 100 square feet of space. In most train stations, this is the kind of window at which red-eyed commuters line up and pay a cheap dollar for an equally cheap cup of coffee, enjoyed for its caffeine not its quality.

But, this is the Winnetka train station, and here train travelers line up to a window for an authentic French baguette, a sweet and flaky almond croissant, a cup of fresh French roasted craft coffee, or all three. Welcome to Cafe Fleurette, where owner Rachel Beaudry offers customers a taste of France along the commuter route of a Chicago suburb.

Beaudry's background takes the shapes, smells, tastes, textures and smells of the art of true French baking. Though never a chef herself, she was married to the co-founder of Chicago's French Pastry School and world-renowned master pastry chef, Jacquie Pfeiffer. Their marriage simultaneously a business partnership, she often acted as the go-to sous chef of the pastry world's best.

A champion of good bread with kept standards, Beaudry found herself dismayed in her Midwestern home in Chicago. Though neither wise nor necessary to compare a real baguette with Wonder bread's finest, what America accepted as French bread pains anyone of serious expertise on the matter. "Americans like their bread under baked," Beaudry explained, a wince nearly audible in her voice. "Good bread comes from good ingredients," she explained, "it can't be super light, it can't be a clunk," rather, it's defined by a "crispy edge, with no big gaping holes," and according to Beaudry, America sorely lacks it.

While Americans enjoy a range of class and category of bread, France protects its boulangerie heritage by governing what may and may not be deemed "French bread." As dictated by Decree No. 93-1074, "*Le Décret Pain*," baked fare of precise size, weight, and appearance made of ingredients held also to specific standards merit the qualification necessary to be called "French bread."[3]

In 2009, Beaudry brought these standards to Chicago's authentic bakery scene by convincing friend and two-time world champion bread maker, Pierre Zimmermann, to leave his 110-year legacy bakery in Schnerscheim, France.[4] With her help, Zimmermann relocated his family to the Windy City and opened La Fournette Bakery and Cafe, bringing the same French bread and pastries from his town of 400 people in Northeastern France to Chicago's Well Street, and one year later, to its Lincoln Park neighborhood.[5]

When Beaudry's two children left for university, Beaudry turned again to her background, passion, skills, and frustration with a general lack of "good bread" in the United States. Zimmermann's successful La Fournette helped ameliorate her city's bread need, but two authentic bakeries could not

---

3   *Décret No. 93-1074 Du 13 Septembre 1993*. 1993. Vol. 2. Paris, France: Official Journal of the French Republic.

4   "La Fournette - French Bakery". 2018. *Lafournette.Com*. Accessed October 12. https://lafournette.com/.

5   Biasco, Paul. 2018. "La Fournette Chef Pierre Zimmermann To Open Lincoln Park Location". *Dnainfo Chicago*. https://www. dnainfo.com/chicago/20130806/lincoln-park/la-fournette-chef-pierre-zimmermann-open-lincoln-park-location/.

be enough for all of Chicago. Beaudry had an idea, Cafe Fleurette.

One hundred square feet of space in her local train station, a location with a hungry audience in desperate need of the sweet delicacies promised by a fresh croissant. The product need not be made on site, simply picked up fresh from Zimmermann in the early hours of the morning—3 a.m. to be exact—before opening—no long-term investment, no hassle in hiring, and no stress of production that would accompany a true brick and mortar establishment. All Beaudry required was a window from which to sell and space to host product for the cafe's four hours of operation every morning, Monday through Saturday, beginning at six o'clock.

"Are you crazy? Who is going to come to the train station for a croissant?" Beaudry's friends would ask. Nearly everyone, as a few months of operation would prove. Not just commuters, but visitors who make it to Chicago's northern Winnetka suburb in a quest for Beaudry's cafe, and a steady stream of locals.

Between the hours of 6:00 a.m. and 10:00 a.m., Beaudry greets loyal customers and daily commuters by name. On Christmas, the little window saw a line of customers filling the station's lobby that diminished only when Beaudry ran out of product at the bitter end of the cafe's operational hours.

On non-holidays, all one hundred and twenty-five of the chocolate croissants and nearly every bread-filled basket will disappear into customer's eager hands. Winnetka residents adore the cafe to such an extent, Beaudry's gym time is no longer sacred. "I'm running on the treadmill and someone will come up to me and ask "can you save me a baguette?".

Neither articles nor paid content can outdo the stamp of local distinction and sincere approval, and Cafe Fluerette flourishes without the aid of media promotion. However, in the age of the internet, a cafe so loved and of such quality cannot not remain a purely local gem.

One *Yelp* reviewer, Kim H., described the cafe:

"*5 stars! A little slice of Paris in Winnetka. Come early, or there will be nothing left. I haven't had anything so delicious in the U.S. Authentic and outstanding in every way. On second thought, stay away! I want to keep this to myself. :)*"[6]

Others echo her praise and warn the spot is "dangerously delicious," recommending readers find a gym membership to defend against Beaudry's croissants.

---

6   "Cafe Fleurette - Winnetka, IL". 2016. *Yelp.* https://www.yelp.com/biz/cafe-fleurette-winnetka?osq=cafe+fluerette.

The headline of one online article is itself a compliment, dubbing the cafe's croissants a "must-try," while a local paper comforts "discerning [Chicago] North Shore Francophiles" in its digital edition, that the search for "the same buttery, melt-in-your-mouth experience" of a croissant from a French boulangerie, "is over."[7, 8] Another local news outlet shares the cafe's accolade as "best local secret."[9] Even student-catered Spoon University joins in the complimentary chatter surrounding the cafe.[10] According to one Northwestern Student, the pistachio macaron is "the French passion for sweets in a nutshell" and with a trip to Beaudry's cafe "you'll be sure to experience a little bit of French perfection sans jet lag."

Media channels were, are, and will continue to be critical tools and forces in the life and income of business owners. Particularly in the food and beverage world, press of any kind will make its mark on the line (or lack thereof) of patrons in the days proceeding. The digital plane has amplified the

---

7   Chang, Chi-an. 2018. "Café Fleurette's Croissant Is A Must Try". *Patch.Com*. https://patch.com/illinois/winnetka/ caf-fleurette-s-croissant-is-a-must-try.

8   Elliott, Libby. 2018. "Small Space, Big Taste In Winnetka Train Station". *Daily North Shore*, , 2018. https://jwcdaily. com/2018/03/04/small-space-big-taste-in-winnetka-train-station/.

9   Maginity, Megan. 2016. "Tucked-Away Café Fleurette Named 'Best Local Secret'". *The Winnetka Current*, , 2016. https://www. winnetkacurrent.com/dining-out/tucked-away-caf%C3%A9-fleurette-named-%E2%80%98best-local-secret%E2%80%99.

10 Lombard, Eilis. 2013. "Café Fleurette". *Spoon University*. https:// spoonuniversity.com/place/cafe-fleurette.

impact of press on profit and expanded the definition of 'media attention' from the printed word to the posted word, inclusive of thrice as many platforms each with an associated demographic.

If an article published on Facebook lauds the lightness of the baguette, Beaudry greets a wave of middle-aged customers. To celebrate Valentine's Day, Cafe Fluerette posted a picture of a tart to Instagram. In the photo, a layer of fresh raspberry preserve hides beneath clouds of chocolate whipped cream with raspberries tucked between and topped with strips of gold-painted chocolate. The photo of it lured crowds of young adults, all of whom are Instagram-savvy. One local newspaper covered Cafe Fleurette in an article, and appealing to a range of readers as good publishers do, released two editions of the article. The digital edition was published online on a Friday while the printed edition hit doorsteps on Saturday morning. Accordingly, Friday's line of baguette buyers were of the multitasking multitudes who read their news while checking email or flick through an article hunched over a phone screen to pass idle time. Saturday's croissant seekers were the sort who, robe-donned, bent down despite presumably stiff joints, to pick up the local paper from the front lawn and flip through its pages with a mug of hot coffee.

Digital acclaim for Cafe Fleurette mixes into the line of regulars, patrons of varying ages and attitudes. Digital food media is a necessary part of Beaudry's business. When prompted to the topic of social media, Beaudry's response was concise but to the point, "You need that platform… you have to be good at social media."

Social media, to Beaudry, rivals if not surpasses the potency of paid advertising, suggesting there really is "no need" for the latter in the face of good, organic publicity shepherded by a strong social following.

"I never had an ad budget, because I never needed an ad budget," she explains. Only once did she hire a food photographer from a local newspaper to create content, but this distinguishes Beaudry from many of her dining industry counterparts. Some restaurant owners live in fear of *Yelp* reviews, studies have quantified the impact of a strong social media standing on profit and guest count, dining industry marketers craft synthesized rubrics for social media well-being, and added to the Internet's treasure trove of "Fails" are restaurants' stained reputations from the likes of *Trip Advisor*, Twitter, Facebook, and Instagram.[11, 12]

---

11   Lutz, Ashley. 2013. "Restaurant Manager Says Yelp Is Killing His Business". *Business Insider*. https://www.businessinsider.com/owner-yelp-is-bad-for-small-business-2013-4.

12   Kim, Woo Gon, Jun (Justin) Li, and Robert A. Brymer. 2016. "The Impact Of Social Media Reviews On Restaurant Performance: The Moderating Role Of Excellence Certificate". *International Journal Of Hospitality Management* 55: 41-51. doi:10.1016/j.ijhm.2016.03.001.

Admittedly, Beaudry herself shies from social media, tentative in her own abilities relative to popular social media mavens. But, buoyed by local celebrity and adoration, and striving to be no grander than a local favorite, Beaudry's cafe rests on the safer side of the Food Internet. The quality of her products and patron's genuine adoration of her product frees her of mandated posts; her success is not contingent on digital glory. Still, the importance of a platform like Instagram to her success is not lost in her uncertainty and she posts on a near daily basis.

The birth of the Food Internet, the sudden explosion of food related media online, shifted the dining industry's relationship with consumers by giving consumers a new platform to interact with food. Neither love for the buttery golden brown flakes of a croissant nor bakery recommendations joyously volunteered are new facets of foodie culture. The Food Internet ushers in a new means of participation and interaction, expanding the dining experience to the digital terrain in which a sincere review is given to anyone scouring *Yelp*, a well-shot Instagram post merits a trip to a new bakery, and a website serves as an establishment's first impression to potential customers.

The interconnectedness of the offline and online worlds reveals itself in Beaudry's 7 a.m. line. A boulangerie tucked into the corner of a commuter train station can expect an entirely different crowd on a Saturday versus a Friday because of the social media page to which a photo or article was posted. The quality of her product ensures the digital dialogue regarding her cafe stays positive and prompts five star reviews but even the certitude of local adoration does not negate the importance of online reputation.

Available to anyone, shared with everyone with no comment, review or headline ever forgotten. Digital food media, the "Food Internet," or another brunching swarm of "kids with their iPhones," this corner of the Internet makes and brakes businesses.

CHAPTER 2

UNCERTAIN TERRAIN

———

Platform is to media what location is to real estate. The perfect home with cutting edge appliances expertly intermingled with soft touches of comfort would be unappealing to any purchaser were it squeezed between the city dump, a six lane highway, and a local paper factory pumping puffs of sulfite and ammonia into the immediate atmosphere.

Accordingly, the best content—rife with color, a potent message, and stunning images—accomplishes little if dependent upon the wrong platform. To those well versed in pillars of advertising and marketing, this is not news. Content that could send people flocking to the establishment in question, means nothing if the desired audience never catches a glimpse.

The media side, the perspective of brands, publishers, or advertisers whose profit depends upon the effective dissemination of and high engagement with content, a degree of dependability is also sought after when defining a perfect platform. The desired demographic can't just be tuned into a platform, the connection ought to be strong. The marketing and media worlds seek the assurance of firm guidelines, codes of conduct that promise their content will not leave a platform, continuously appearing before the right eyes.

Regarding the Food Internet, social media is generally agreed to be the best neighborhood. Though limited to sound, image, and the suggestions of friends and family, the content of the Food Internet brings all the lushness and warmth of food itself. Pictures of matcha green lattes or the cheddar-yellow of hot macaroni and cheese color this digital corner, YouTube cooking shows never fail to miss the searing hiss of a stir fry, and all of which made oh so easily sent to family, friends, or with whomever else one chooses to dine. The vibrancy and community of food is matched by the capabilities of social media, and every social media user, if not an associate of foodie culture, is a diner.

To add to its potential, Twitter, Snapchat, YouTube, Instagram, and other social media platforms offer industry actors the tools to monitor their content. Once successfully uploaded and disseminated, the reach and rates of engagement from specific content may be observed and improved as needed according to the advertising or publisher guidelines offered by the platforms.

From among the list of social media platforms, Facebook is both prime and reasonable real estate; a beachfront property or penthouse apartment with a comfortable (even under budget) price tag. Compatible with colorful content varying from videos or articles? Check. Easily placed in front of and shared amongst the right audience? Check. Confidence in clearly outlined code of conducts and platform support? Check. Until about a year ago.

In January of 2018, when I began writing this book, Facebook changed and the media industry shook. The platform announced two major alterations:

- The News Feed algorithm now prioritized content from family and friends, rather than from publishers
- Its Branded Content Guidelines adjusted as to prohibit the exchange of "anything of value" for sharing content that the page owners did not themselves create

These changes improved user-experience, but stripped commercial users of their arsenal. The methods publishers, advertisers, and brands had come to rely upon meant nothing under these new rulings. Their faith in Facebook and their consequential confidence in their own ability to reach an audience, gone.

These changes also came in the midst of a global distrust in social media, large corporations, and online content. Fearing fake news and well aware that personal information did not belong to the person, Facebook's changes aimed to soothe these public aches, weeding out fake news and fraudulent ads and advancing the news feed ratio of news to personal posts in favor of people, families, and communities. Facebook turned its back on publishers and advertisers to face, instead, the individual user.

"There's a feeling that we're in the middle of a reckoning," said Grant Whitmore, an evp at Tronc, the Chicago-based print and online media publishing company, as quoted by Digiday.[13]

In the following weeks, the journalists at the digital marketing and advertising publisher, DigiDay, wrote article after article forecasting ominous futures for those who had regarded Facebook as their critical, if not primary, tool. The website warned readers of a "new reality" in the digital media

---

13 Moses, Lucia. 2018. "'We're In The Middle Of A Reck-
     oning': At Digital Media Gathering, New Reality Sets
     In - Digiday". *Digiday*. https://digiday.com/marketing/
     reality-sets-in-at-ad-execs-annual-meeting/.

sphere and, reflecting the sentiments of the media industry, inserted Facebook CEO and Founder, Mark Zuckerberg's face to the center of a fiery mushroom cloud.

In February, Digiday contributor Max Willens quotes the founder of one company that had used the newly banned distribution model: "Gone are the days when social publishers enjoyed relatively cheap distribution of their low quality content through influencer pages."[14] That article was titled "Facebook's New Branded-Content Guidelines will Force Some Publishers to Abandon a Business Model."[15] Then in March, Digiday published the article: "One-time social publishing star Cooking Panda is shutting down."[16]

* * *

A light green icon with a gleeful cartoon panda donning a chef's hat waves from the homepage of a green and black colored website. Credited as one of the first platforms to help popularize the "hands-in-pans" style of video, Cooking

---

14 Willens, Max. 2018. "Facebook's New Branded-Content Guidelines Will Force Some Publishers To Abandon A Business Model - Digiday". *Digiday*. https://digiday.com/media/facebooks-new-branded-content-guidelines-will-force-publishers-abandon-business-model/.

15 Moses. "'We're In The Middle Of A Reckoning': At Digital Media Gathering, New Reality Sets In - Digiday". *Digiday*.

16 Moses, Lucia. 2018. "Onetime Social Publishing Star Cooking Panda Is Shutting Down - Digiday". *Digiday*. https://digiday.com/media/onetime-social-publishing-star-cooking-panda-shutting/.

Panda was a social-first recipe video publisher founded in 2010.[17]

The same Panda waves from the left hand corner of Cooking Panda's website, inviting readers to indulge themselves in "Mouthwatering Pizza GIFs" whose thumbnail features four full-grown adults holding their drinks in one hand while helping themselves to the corner of a pizza that takes up the entirety of their table. The transparent grey play button floats over the words "Inside-Out Grilled Cheese" stretching diagonally across the screen in all caps as anonymous hands pull apart what can only be the gooey goodness of the "inside-out grilled cheese." This is Cooking Panda—not unlike the other publishers dominating the Food Internet and food porn world but, smaller. Publishing video recipes, cartoons and lifestyle content, Cooking Panda was more than social-first, it was Facebook first, and there it earned the majority of its views.[18]

Its Facebook cover photo is not a photo but a montage of Cooking Panda's miraculous feats of indulgence—a strawberry rises from a sea of chocolate, a steady stream of maple syrup washes over a tower of pancakes missing a triangular slice, an enormous serving of pasta smothered in an orange sauce, a steak is flipped on a grill sending a puff of smoke

17   Ibid.
18   Ibid.

towards the camera, and someone pulls a french fry from a smothering mass of gravy, cheese, herbs, and of course, bacon. A little line of icons advertise Cooking Panda's apps and platforms, barely noticeable against the gluttonous reel behind.

This page made Cooking Panda.

A subsidiary of Render Media, once named the second fastest growing American media company by *Inc. Magazine*, Cooking Panda had grown its Facebook fans from 700,000 to 5.3million in a single year.[19] Then, it had boasted higher engagement rates than industry giants like *Tasty* and *Tastemade*. Videos like "Jalapeño Popper Stuffed Bacon Chicken" attracted 25 million viewers with a glimpse into the layers of browned bacon wound around tender chicken, encircling a jalapeño stuffed with cheese.[20] Thousands more watched the "Fried Ice Cream" video in whose thumbnail vanilla ice cream drips melts down the side of a broken sphere of fried, chocolate drizzled, whipped cream and mint topped fried ice

---

19   "Render Media Honored In The Top 2% Of The 2016 Inc. 5000 List". 2018. *Prnewswire.Com*. https://www.prnewswire.com/ news-releases/render-media-honored-in-the-top-2-of-the 2016-inc-5000-list-300316076.html.

20   Cooking Panda. 2018. *Jalapeño Popper Stuffed Bacon Chicken*. Video. https://www.facebook.com/MrCookingPanda/ videos/1790536324304385/.

cream serving.[21] The future looked bright for Cooking Panda. Then, Facebook prohibited third-party content, stopping a main source of Cooking Panda's income, and changed its algorithm to promote posts from family and friends, not Cheddar Bacon Chicken Ranch Pasta.[22]

Between December and January, Cooking Panda's video views fell to 2.5 million—half of its previous viewership.[23] In March of 2018, word was out: Cooking Panda and all of Render Media was closing shop.

"The combined impact of several recent events have severely restricted Render's cash flow and its ability to sustain its business," Render Media wrote in a note to its clients.[24] Among these reasons, Render highlighted Facebook's changes to its branded content guideline, which diminished support from its partner-publishing network. The company's spokeswoman emphasized the adjustment to the Facebook news-

---

21   Cooking Panda. 2018. *Fried Ice Cream*. Video. https://www.facebook.com/MrCookingPanda/videos/1873363382688345/.

22   Cooking Panda. 2018. *Cheddar Bacon Chicken Ranch Pasta*. Video. https://www.facebook.com/MrCookingPanda/videos/1900372163320800/.

23   Moses. "Onetime Social Publishing Star Cooking Panda Is Shutting Down - Digiday". *Digiday*.

24   Mullin, Benjamin. 2018. "Cooking Panda Owner Is The Latest Digital Publisher To Shut Down After Facebook Changes". *WSJ*. https://www.wsj.com/articles/cooking-panda-owner-is-the-latest-digital-publisher-to-shut-down-after-facebook-changes-1522277679.

feed algorithm to prioritize local content and posts from friends and family over click-bait and commercial content.

Other larger publishers and media companies, like *Tasty* and *Tastemade*, felt the rumblings of the platform's shift. Unfortunately, what was a simple tremor for them, was earth shattering for Cooking Panda. Facebook dependency had claimed a casualty, and the small publisher that gave digital media giants such as Tasty and *Tastemade* a run for their money, lost.

Before Digiday released their article covering Cooking Panda's collapse, Max Willens of Digiday had watched Cooking Panda long before its fall. He noted when the platform began diversifying its content, offering cooking classes and subscription, as many publishers have in the wake of a saturated recipe video market, but when Willens wrote about a forcibly abandoned business model, he predicted Cooking Panda's demise.

"It's hard for folks like that to find a way to survive if they can't diversify their distributions past Facebook," Willens explains. Their freshly cut supply of referral traffic would be hard to replace "there's nothing else out there that delivers on that scale," and " video content, food video content doesn't travel well," he continued. The shortfall of Cooking Panda's business model was of no great surprise.

* * *

The life and death of Cooking Panda warns of the dangers about over dependency on a single platform. By no means was Cooking Panda the only entity to perceive Facebook as ground firm enough to shape a business model around. Any publisher who depended on Facebook as a means of disseminating news or content was forced to recalibrate their efforts. What saved others was diversification, the deeper roots of a legacy brand, or a strongly supported company could overcome such a change.

Survival in the months following Facebook's announcements in January of 2018 is not indication of sturdy ground. In an interview from July of 2018, Jonah Peretti, BuzzFeed's CEO and founder, criticized the nature of the relationship between Facebook and companies like BuzzFeed:

"When media got to a huge scale on those platforms, it seemed to make sense that they would find ways to share revenue with people creating so much value for their platforms. YouTube has done an okay job. With Facebook, we have examples like Tasty, where we are the biggest franchise on Facebook, and we generate zero revenue from Facebook."[25]

25   Sangal, Aditi. 2018. "Buzzfeed'S Jonah Peretti: 'We'Ve Proven We Can Be Profitable'". Podcast. *Digiday Podcast*. https://digiday.com/podcast/digiday-podcast-jonah-peretti-buzzfeed-facebook/.

We are the biggest franchise on Facebook and we generate zero revenue from Facebook. Not even BuzzFeed has it entirely figured out.

Peretti's quote makes evident the widespread angst surrounding social media platforms in the media industry. Frustration with Facebook pervades even the BuzzFeed Empire. What is more, the changes Facebook announced at the year's start are not isolated incidents of change in the realm of social media.

Facebook continues to change, tweaking the ecosystem between itself, its publishers, and its users. Abroad, the EU's General Data Protection Regulation, implemented in late May of 2018 alters how advertisers target and reach audiences. Not to mention the ne'er ceasing flow of updates to other social media platforms such as the introduction of Instagram Watch, the ability to follow a hashtag, Snapchat's redesign, and countless more that will inevitably occur by the time of this book's publication.

I asked nearly every individual interviewed for this book a variant of the same question: What works? What's the secret to navigating social media? Have you figured it out? The answer was a resounding, "No, we have not figured it out nor will we—the challenge is new every day."

The standard social media has set for its commercial side is that of inconsistency and whiplash. Ever modified, ever upgrading, and ever multiplying as audiences' fragmented attention spreads across numerous platforms. The motives and demographics of those who spend their time on Instagram versus Facebook or Snapchat or simply subscribe to email newsletters vary. Those users again splinter off into interest-specific sub-communities and each served a different round of content. We exist in an age where the headlines I see on the *New York Times'* homepage differ from that of my neighbor or my sister or my colleague when they land on the same address. Our digital common ground disappears before us while media businesses struggle to sew together a permanent and growing following.

With the internet weighing as it is on food media, those navigating it lack the certainty of consistency and suffer the symptoms of whiplash, ever bouncing across digital channels and between the real world. No conduct guidelines can be cemented as the truth. Rather, certitude rests in understanding what lures people to this side of the internet. Why has food flourished as it has on the digital plane, and what greater purpose can an Instagram post or Facebook article serve?

Grasp what is precious about this content. Sew its pieces together by knowing what ought to be celebrated and promoted across content, platforms, and sub-communities. Read on.

PART II

ACCESS

*"What I say is that, if a fellow really likes potatoes, he must be
a pretty decent sort of fellow."*

—A. A. MILNE

Take the pulse of the cooking and dining world as it stands,
who and what do you find?

Is it Dave Chang? The celebrity chef whose career first came
about from ramen bowls and pork buns, settled on the name
"Momofuku" due in part to its similarity to "motherf* * * *r"

and his favorite beer is Bud Light because its "shitty beer."[26, 27] Dessert-inclined readers may think, instead, of Chang's counterpart Christina Tosi, the woman behind Momofuku Milk Bar, who "think[s] the world is more often your oyster when you approach it with more of a childlike sensibility," and whose cereal-milk soft serve or and unfrosted birthday cakes aim to share that simple sensibility.[28] Perhaps its Guy Fieri, the television personality and restaurateur best known for sharing the casual greatness of America's *Diners, Drive-Ins and Dives*. Maybe your mind drifts downheartedly the loss of two greats in the food world— Jonathan Gold and Anthony Bourdain. Gold, a champion of the Los Angeles food landscape whose work was colored by the traditional international cuisines and recognized with a Pulitzer Prize, passed in July mere weeks after Bourdain in the Summer of 2018.

The world grieved loudly for Bourdain. People, who never opened the "Food" section of the newspaper, or made reservations months in advance for the city's most requested

26 Roberts, Daniel. 2018. "David Chang Broke All The Rules | TIME.Com". *TIME.Com*. http://business.time.com/2013/09/26/ david-chang-broke-all-the-rules/.

27 Chang, David. 2018. "David Chang's Kitchen: My Name Is David Chang, And I Hate Fancy Beer". *GQ*. https://www.gq.com/story/ david-chang-cheap-beer.

28 Fuhrmeister, Chris. 2018. "'Chef's Table: Pastry' Recap: Christina Tosi Channeled Her Childlike Wonder Into A Dessert Empire". *Eater*. https://www.eater.com/2018/4/13/17230656/ chefs-table-pastry-christina-tosi-recap-episode-1.

tables, suffered the pangs of loss. People who had only seen a glimpse of his show or read a single article, people of all positions, industries, backgrounds, and nationalities, people everywhere were saddened by news of his death and the end of Bourdain's raw, rebellious, but impassioned perspective.

Before his own passing, Gold responded to Bourdain's death in an L.A. Times article, *"Anthony Bourdain opened the working-class kitchen to the world and the world to us:"*

"...his first book, *Kitchen Confidential*, slashed through the walls separating working-class cooks from their soft, well-fed customers, and for perhaps the first time since George Orwell's *Down and Out in Paris and London*, elevated the rough humanity of the kitchen above the soft pleasures of the table... Bourdain looked for answers about the future of places such as Libya, Ethiopia, and the Punjab region of India through their food cultures...I cannot imagine how the food world is going to cope with this gaping Bourdain-shaped hole—not at its center but on its fringes, looking exactly like a man throwing rocks at the status quo."[29]

29 Gold, Jonathan. 2018. "Anthony Bourdain opened the work-ing-class kitchen to the world and the world to us". *Latimes.Com.* http://www.latimes.com/food/jonathan-gold/la-fo-gold-anthony-bourdain-20180608-story.html.

A wall-slashing, door breaking, Bourdain created access. He threw back the curtain on kitchens and spoke equally for the anonymous men and women behind fine dining's swinging doors as a pho shop in the middle of Hanoi.[30] Like Gold, Bourdain did not restrain his palate to the white table clothed and critically acclaimed.

The culinary world Bourdain and Gold revealed, others continued. Phil Rosenthal, the mind behind *Everybody Loves Raymond*, pitched his food and travel show to Netflix, *Somebody Feed Phil,* with the words: "'I'm exactly like Anthony Bourdain if he was afraid of everything...I mean, I'm the guy watching him, not really wanting to go to Borneo and have a tattoo pounded into my chest with nails.'"[31]

With this adventurous timidity, *Somebody Feel Phil's* first season begins with what Rosenthal dubs, "Earth's greatest hits," because the "goal of the show is to get you to travel, Mr. Sit in your chair and never move, and like only what you like," because, as Rosenthal explains, "...if you see Paris, if you see Florence, if you see Barcelona. And if you see how accessible it is, and you see lots of other Americans are going

---

30 Bourdain, Anthony. 2010. *Medium Raw: A Bloody Valentine To The World Of Food And The People Who Cook*. 1st ed. New York: HarperCollins Publishers.

31 Serious Eats. 2018. "Phil Rosenthal Is Anthony Bourdain Except Afraid Of Everything". Podcast.

too, maybe that'll be your first step."[32] Employing the "if I can, you can too" argument with wide eyes, collared shirts and smiles that push the limits of Rosenthal's mouth, he too opens the world through food.[33]

A Google search or Snapchat story from the other side of the globe as ordinary as breakfast, the world weaves ever more tightly together. About three quarters of U.S. adults use YouTube and the average American reports using three of eight major platforms.[34] Online, people form communities, learn about the world, and find new space for their own voice and these opportunities are offered anyone with enough bandwidth to create an account.

This is the world in which Bourdain, Gold, and Rosenthal made names for themselves. Is it of any great surprise then that we think of the "anti-restaurant" Chang when we think of food celebrities? That we celebrate Tosi's unassuming desserts? That traditional foods and international flavors have shifted our palettes?

The internet and an accessible food scene—perhaps it's a modern, though less catchy, version of the chicken or egg

---

32 Ibid.
33 Ibid.
34 Smith, Aaron, and Monica Anderson. 2018. "Social Media Use 2018". Pew Research Center. http://www.pewinternet. org/2018/03/01/social-media-use-in-2018/.

question. While Rosenthal Face Times his parents, someone googles what restaurants Bourdain visited while he too was in Argentina. Someone else adds another photo of cereal milk ice cream to Instagram, and someone else posts to one of Chang's online fan pages, and yet someone else swallows a dry lump in her throat before posting her own #MeToo experience from years in the restaurant industry.

Open-source, inclusive, public, accessible—call it what you will, but the food scene of today and the Internet keep at heart the common man from the world at large.

CHAPTER 3

EVERYONE'S A FOODIE

___

#food appears on 292million posts and counting, on Instagram. Type "Best Instagram influencers" into Google and you'll get 3,710,000 results in less than half a second.

"The 40 Food Instagram Accounts You Should Be Following Right Now" by *Food & Wine* and "12 Foodie Instagram Accounts You Seriously Should Follow" by BuzzFeed target the unspecialized food lover. "18 Foodie Instagram Accounts Every Serious Cook Should Follow" exists for those embarking on their own culinary endeavors, *Saveur* annually publishes its list of the best food Instagrams along with a list of its "Favorite Vegan Instagrams" and a handful of month-specific lists of the "Global Food Photos We Loved." Business Insider too is in on the action. While Spoon University went so far as to publish "These 8 Food Instagram Accounts Are the Opposite of Food Porn" featuring an account that only documents airplane food, an account that Photoshops pictures of Meryly Streep onto different dishes, and an account that scavenges for and posts the least appetizing food photos the Internet has to offer. No food is unwelcome and nearly everyone is participating.

Articles from the BBC and numerous other news outlets claim Instagram is "changing the way we eat."[35] One study reports roughly "half of Americans Take pictures of their food" prompting all corners of the culinary world—from the home chef to the professional—to chase standards of 'Instagram-ability.'[36]

Ali Corwin works for a think tank in Washington, D.C. She has brown hair and brown eyes. She graduated from the University of Michigan with a Masters Degree in Management only a few years ago, and as she puts it, she likes "podcasts, coffee, and people watching. Oh! And I love serial killer documentaries."

35 Tandoh, Ruby. 2016. "Click Plate: How Instagram Is Changing The Way We Eat". *The Guardian*. https://www.theguardian.com/lifeandstyle/2016/nov/02/click-plate-how-instagram-changing-way-we-eat-food.

36 McCarthy, Niall. 2018. "Infographic: Half Of Americans Take Pictures Of Their Food". *Statista Infographics*. https://www.statista.com/chart/12776/half-of-americans-take-pictures-of-their-food/.

A typical day is "wake up, go to work come home" then prepare to do it all again the next day. Of course, a Michigan or Falcons football game may upset the neat order of her routine but on a week-by-week basis, Corwin lives the life of a typical twenty-something, living in or around the D.C. metro area.

Accordingly, Corwin would brand herself as a foodie.

The word 'foodie' first appeared in print in 1980, written by former *New York* magazine food critic Gael Greene, and was more popularly coined by journalists Ann Barr and Paul Levy who released *The Official Foodie Handbook* four years afterwards.[37] Then, the authors defined a foodie as "a person who is very, very, very interested in food."[38] A version of 'epicure,' an adjective for those with a then-niche interest and above average knowledge base. But following Barr and Levy's publication, that group of people grew—a lot.

When Filipino restaurateur, Elbert Cuenca, was asked about the word he claimed:

37 Ferdman, Roberto A. 2016. "Stop Calling Yourself A 'Foodie'". *Washington Post*. https://www.washingtonpost.com/news/wonk/wp/2016/03/01/why-the-word-foodie-is-terrible-and-needs-to-go-away/?noredirect=on&utm_term=.e12c25950f6c.

38 Ferdman. 2016. "Stop Calling Yourself A 'Foodie'". *Washington Post*.

"It has come to the point of being bastardized. The word 'foodie,' which is nothing more than a modern-day casual substitute for 'gourmet,' has been relegated to mean anyone who likes food and/or eats out a lot. But who doesn't like food? Who doesn't eat out a lot?"[39]

And in even more recent times, the definition has gained a digital edge. A 19 year old interviewed in a Spoon University article defined foodie as, "Someone who posts excessive amounts of food pictures on social media accounts and will drive 3 hours to eat a single *cronut*."[40] The 'bastardized' word, its association with social-media's food porn craze, and mere overuse has been to the chagrin and frustration of the culinary world, but its widespread popularity remains. Today, nearly everyone is a "foodie."

Corwin follows @Dcfoodporn, she once posted a picture of ice cream she had in Fort Meyers, Florida and she enjoys a good meal out. She qualifies by the general and contemporary standards of 'foodie'-ism, and as such, ultimately chooses a restaurant based on her company, her hunger, what's nearby and what is within budget. So, when Corwin went out to dinner with her fellow Midwestern roommate and closest

---

39   Ibid.
40   McCurry Hahn, Saoirse. 2017. "I Asked 9 People To Define The Term "Foodie" And Their Answers Were Surprisingly Different". *Spoon University*. https://spoonuniversity.com/lifestyle/9-people-offer-their-own-definitions-of-the-term-foodie.

friend in October of 2017, they chose a restaurant not based on extravagance or Michelin stars, but on a single, simple craving—queso.

D.C. offers its turophiles dishes ranging from Compass Rose's khachapuri, the Georgian specialty that resembles a bread boat of melted cheese encasing a single egg, to a beloved bubbling skillet of queso fundido offered at a number of local restaurants. Corwin and her friends were in search of something far simpler.

"There's the Mexican restaurant in every hometown that's not authentic but it's just cheesy—no pun intended." Corwin explains. The kind of place that splashes bursts of purple and red decor on walls painted to look like stucco. Where the entire wait staff bring out a sombrero and sing an English, mariachi style version of Happy Birthday on your special day. Queso, at this kind of Mexican restaurant, is of a particular sort.

"It's this thin smooth white dip and it's the best," Corwin describes. Corwin and her friends searched for this Americanized delicacy—not freshly imported from Mexico that morning, not decked with meat and strange spices, but something that tasted perfectly, inauthetnically, of hometowns.

Neither a town nor overly populated with inauthentic cuisine, and pressured by an international audience, D.C.'s culinary scene strays from touristy dips that film over on top when cool and untouched for too long a period. Still, the white cheesy dip sings nostalgically of home to the hearts and roots of some of its imported residents.

The queso Corwin and her group ordered in October fell short of their hopes for the hometown version they craved. Perhaps not pale enough or too easily identified as real cheese, the version they received revealed a lack in D.C.'s dining and gave rise to an idea. Their disappointment snowballed into a mission; a quest to find the queso they imagined and craved. Their experience photographed and documented on the Food Internet's favorite social media platform.

On October 16, 2017 the Instagram account @bitches_quest_4_queso was created and published its first post.[41] A dark photo shows a freshly served enchilada flanked by piles of rice, guacamole, and a cup of the unsatisfying queso glowing in the crimson-hued light. The inaugural caption read as follows:

"Hello Washington. Thank you for allowing us to become your gurus for everything queso in this city. Unfortunately

---

41   2017. Blog. *@Bitches_Quest_4_Queso.* https://www.instagram.com/bitches_quest_4_queso/.

(for all of us,) dc is not Mecca for those searching for spiritual healing via white cheesy dip. To start off, here is an attempt by *(not including name)* in Southeast. Still not up to par.... but stay tuned; we promise better will come!"

Not food porn of the city's many photogenic dishes, but an account based on discovery and display of a single, arguably unoriginal dish. Pictures of chips arising from tiny yellow and white hued seas populate the account alongside D.C.'s nacho offerings. Organic and casual, the account is a dairy diary of sorts for friends and followers of the three founding "bitches."

At this point in writing, the account has gathered over one thousand followers with 48 total posts. Corwin, who does a majority of the posting, only gives the account an hour or two of attention per week. Though the group has certainly been invited by restaurants for an on-the-house queso tasting, the members' decisions to try a restaurant motive a post, not the other way around.

The Instagram foodie community has influencers, people paid to take pictures and post about their meals. These accounts claim thousands of followers who drool over colorful images of meals posted with a brilliant eye for the sort of aesthetics that appeal to the connection between eye and stomach.

The "bitches" questing for queso are not of this branch. They join sincere cravings with an average voice and no theatrics. Their account reflects the focused voice of an average foodie. Though treated to the occasional comp'ed queso and chips, Corwin and her friends' behaviors differ little from their peers. They enjoy food and dining out, their opinions are not shaped by an extensive culinary education or highly refined palette, but still they participate, casting their thoughts and devoured dishes into the digital public eye.

British food critic and journalist, John Lanchester's words hold true:

"Everyone's a critic, they say, and that's certainly true of the food world today. Of course, everyone has always been a critic, in the sense that customers have always made the most basic judgment of all: Do I want to come back to this joint? But there's a contemporary development with respect to volume, in the dual sense of quantity and loudness. The volume of all this critical chatter is turned way up, and it's harder than ever to ignore."[42]

About half of Americans participate in this chatter. Perhaps less, but perhaps more, and moving forward, perhaps even more.

---

42   Lanchester, John. 2014. "Shut Up And Eat". *The New Yorker*. https://www.newyorker.com/magazine/2014/11/03/shut-eat.

According to a statistic by *Bon Appetit*, millennials, the youngest working cohort, spend over $96 billion a year on food—roughly 14 times as much as the average middle class family.[43] With 85-89% of millennials on Facebook and 59% active Instagram users, they drive up the millions of hits for the Instagram hashtag #yum.[44] As they settle into adulthood, the digital-native Generation Z (aka the iGeneration) begins to graduate from college, emerging as consumers and creators who expect the Food Internet and were not around for the days before *Yelp*, and Snapchat's Food porn Fridays.

* * *

The Internet has millions of pasta dish recipes. From "45 Easy Pasta Dinner Recipes" collected by *Country Living* to homemade linguine for Gaida De Lauretiis's Chicken Tetrazzini five-star recipe, backed by 1200 reviews.[45]

But what if you're a college freshman still chained to a meal plan? Or if you only bought microwave mac and cheese but

43 Peele, Anna. 2016. "Just How Food-Obsessed Is The Typical Millennial?". *Bon Appetit*. https://www.bonappetit.com/entertaining-style/pop-culture/article/millennials-and-food.

44 Fuscaldo, Donna. 2017. "Instagram: 59% Of U.S. Millennials Are Active Users". *Investopedia*. https://www.investopedia.com/news/instagram-59-us-millennials-are-active-users/.

45 De Laurentiis, Giada. 2018. "Chicken Tetrazzini | Recipes". *Foodnetwork.Com*. Accessed October 13. https://www.foodnetwork.com/recipes/giada-de-laurentiis/chicken-tetrazzini-recipe-1943960.

the only microwave is the one in the common room, known to spark, and still bearing the scorch marks from the Friday someone left a metal fork in takeout they were reheating? What if you want to splurge outside of the dining hall but don't know what off-campus restaurant is really worth your parent's hard earned money? Then Spoon University, the Food Internet conglomerate geared for its youngest users, is for you.

The homepage of Spoon University, a subset of Scripps Network, opens with any combination of Trader Joe's tips and tricks, Color Changing Gin, 8 Back to School Breakfast Ideas for Busy College Students and 'How-To' videos catered to the college student's budget, appliances, and palette.[46, 47] Self described, Spoon University is "The food resource for our generation… featuring recipes, restaurant reviews, personal stories and hacks to help you 'adult'".

The right hand corner of the page encourages one to "Find Your Campus," and brings the visitor to a list, hundreds of names long, of college campuses across the United States

46   Conley, Ellie. 2018. "Color Changing Gin Exists, And It Will Make Your Gin & Tonic Turn Pink". *Spoon University*. https://spoonuniversity.com/lifestyle/color-changing-gin-exists-and-it-will-upgrade-your-gin-and-tonic.

47   Orr, Cassidy. 2018. "8 Back To School Breakfast Ideas For Busy College Students". *Spoon University*. https://spoonuniversity.com/lifestyle/8-back-to-school-breakfast-ideas-for-busy-college-students.

and world, including Australia's Canberra University.[48] Each campus, or "chapter," of the SpoonU community is run by that chapter's students and tailors its content to its local readership.

Campus-specific pages include location-agnostic articles like "Zoodle" recipes and incredible insight into Kylie Jenner's top pregnancy craving (Eggo waffles, apparently), alongside neighborhood-relevant features. For example, the Georgetown University page covers the arrival of the "Amazingly Basic" Bluestone Lane DC , the University of Michigan page features "The MDining Changes You Need to Know About" and College of Charleston makes sure to include "The 4 Best Bagel Sandwiches in Charleston".[49] Some chapters are larger or more established than others but the lure remains: the Food Internet for and by its largest audience.

Spoon is "a global community of young influencers shaping the future of food" as Georgetown University is a "tight knit [community] of remarkable individuals interested

---

48   "Find Your Campus". 2018. *Spoonuniversity.Com*. https://spoon-university.com/campuses.

49   "Spoon University | The Food Resource For Our Generation". 2018. *Spoonuniversity.Com*. Accessed October 14. https://spoon-university.com/.

in intellectual inquiry and making a difference in the world."[50, 51] Though community significantly affects the experience, students attend Georgetown and similar institutions for the education and opportunity. Spoon aims to "teach the next generation of journalists, marketers, and event planners in digital media"—holding fast to the 'university' facet of its nomenclature, and offering for the youngest generation an education and community, fused.

This union inspired Olivia Frzop to start the Butler University SpoonU chapter. Frzop was founder and as Photo Director for her chapter, managing four other Butler University students who also contribute to Spoon. The group of five wrote stories and articles, kept up the SpoonU Butler Instagram, and filled the chapter with bright photos of ice cream piled into and dripping over the sides of a waffle cone.

Each week, Frzop spent hours editing photos, piecing together content and coordinating what written articles would be paired with what photo. Over video chats, she checked in with her advisor at HQ alongside a handful of other SpoonU chapter directors. Together, they exchanged ideas, rarely heard the word "no" from the advisor, and conclude

---

50   "The Food Resource For Our Generation". 2018. *Spoonuniversity. Com.* https://spoonuniversity.com/about.

51   "Admissions & Aid". 2018. *Georgetown.Edu.* Accessed October 13. https://www.georgetown.edu/admissions.

meetings secure in the fact that each chapter's operations are left almost entirely to the hands of the students.

Frzop and her colleagues are autonomous, but in training. She has a high quality camera and is well versed in photography but Spoon further trained Fzrop. SpoonU's headquarters passed on tips about the iPhone camera light adjustment slider, which pops up when you hold down the screen, and the best angles from which to photograph different kinds of food. SpoonU is there to provide a structure, a platform, and resources.

Spoon University's traffic leaped from 200,000 unique visitors to 2 million between February and April of 2015 alone, and by the fall of 2016, it captured roughly 4 million unique visitors per month.[52] The list of participating chapters continues to expand, developed equally by the hungry student looking for a campus-cooking tip as by the photography student eager to exercise his or her skills on a popular platform.

Students study how to take the best video of a poached egg alongside the philosophies of Aristotle or the basics of International Economics. The eagerness by which students

---

52 Paul, Eve. 2018. "How To Manage Millennials? Spoon University Cracked The Code And Is Reaping The Rewards". *Forbes*. https://www.forbes.com/sites/eveturowpaul/2016/11/21/how-to-manage-millennials-spoon-university-cracked-the-code-and-is-reaping-the-rewards/.

across the globe have established and contributed to their SpoonU chapters, can only anticipate a growing future of digital food media.

Corwin and Frzop represent young, but contemporary members. Open to anyone with internet access and an appetite, the 'foodie' contingent continues to grow.

CHAPTER 4

NEW CHANNELS

———

In my childhood household, my parents ruled the remote. If the remote fell specifically to my father's hands, the television filled our kitchen and living rooms with the sounds of HGTV or the Food Network.

With three children no more than four years apart in the house, I applaud my father for his stubbornness. The risk of rebellion against hours of home remodels and house flips or restaurant exploration and cooking competitions was inevitable every time he tore us from the Disney Channel. Yet he persisted, firm in his preference and stern in his decision to take back the television from our elementary school gang. What say we had in the matter was a choice between two evils, real estate or reduction sauce? Carpentry or caramelized onions? House Hunters or Alton Brown?

My friends at school relayed the same saga, cartoons torn away from greedy eyes and replaced with something with far fewer high-pitched voices and bathroom jokes. Guy Fieri, Giada De Laurentiis, Bobby Flay, Rachael Ray—we begrudgingly watched them all. These were the faces to whom the adults of my childhood looked toward to master home-cooked macaroni and cheese in a valiant effort to upgrade from the blue and orange boxes my siblings and I routinely demanded.

The Food Network existed for them- the parents, the home-owners, the comfortably settled adults. It existed for the people who could take the remote back from young hands on the basis of owning the TV and paying for cable. For those of us without the buying power to purchase a banana—let alone a TV—or the heavy burden of grocery shopping for a house-hold, the Food Network was something we listened to and perhaps secretly enjoyed but it was not for us. It was not *our* channel. This is not to say we were uninterested in meals and cooking and food, but we tuned our eyes and ears elsewhere.

* * *

In 2009, Frankie Celenza's degree in Recorded Music from NYU's Tisch was one project away from comple-tion. Extended family in Italy had offered Celenza the per-fect excuse to take Italian and spend his summers abroad, fulfilling his humanities requirement in Southern Italy's sloping landscapes. Time with Italian family comes, of course, with authentic Italian cooking. Learning to cook with the unmeasured "quanto basto" or "correct amount" of ingredients beneath a family member's watchful eye, supplemented Celenza's spoken Italian practice.[53] With each flight back to New York City, Celenza found himself missing more than the Italian countryside and his relatives. He missed cooking.

"It was a 'you don't know what you got till it's gone'" sort of attachment Celenza describes from those return flights. "Each summer my spoken Italian would improve and each school year I'd host dinner parties for my classmates, teaching them the stories I'd learned about each dish," Celenza explained. Slowly, slowly, he recognized his connection to cooking growing into "love," a passion to be pursued and preserved despite the many miles between New York and Italy.

From his open-facing kitchen, Celenza carried his guests through the entirety of a dish, with the gusto of the entertainer he was studying to be. Delighted, full, and better educated on the history of spaghetti and meatballs, Celenza's

---

53 Celenza, Frankie. 2018. "Italian-American Food Never Claimed To Be Italian, So You Can Stop Hating On It". *Huffpost Life*. https://www.huffpost.com/entry/ italian-american-food_n_5b364d53e4b08c3a8f69c37c.

friends and guests began echoing the same phrase "you should start your own food web show."

"After I'd heard this suggestion from about ten different people, I knew I had to give it a shot," Celenza explains, and in the initial form of a capstone project, *Frankie Cooks* began.

"On the surface it seems funny that my {recorded music} capstone was a cooking show, but all its elements are parallel to the creation, branding and selling of music… When I film a show, it's a performance," In the recent "6 Minute Penne" episode, Celenza holds true to this. He holds a lemon before the camera, breaking the quick pulse of the show to describe what great advantage the slivers of rind cut moments later hold over their zested versions. He looks at an oversized clock in feigned fret to see if the recipe will indeed take the mere six minutes he promised his viewers, and holds a steaming forkful of penne pasta to the camera with four seconds to spare. To tell the story of Polenta, Celenza appears in the heavy layers of knitted beige clothing and mopped wig of grey fastened with a kerchief appropriate for an Italian grandmother. *Frankie Cooks* follows in the footsteps of its Food Network muses, but breaks tradition in its mode and manner.

Celenza takes the sounds of cooking—the crunch of chopping onions and the explosive sizzle between fresh meat and hot oil, and amplifies them:

"When I'm editing the show, I spend hundreds of hours each month in the edit suite, it's no different than a late night at the console in studio 505 trying to manipulate a section until it's just right," Celenza writes in Tisch's alumni spotlight.[54] "I need to have an incredible grasp of the current state of camera and microphone equipment in order to push the boundaries of what's technically possible and new."

Pushing those boundaries even further, Celenza pairs each recipe's steps with music that echoes the recipe's development. "Since your television doesn't have smell-vision, I'm going to tickle your other senses with the music that's composed for the dish," a young Celenza says at the start of a "Behind the Scenes" video from 2010. A drum rasps in time with Celenza's hand smashing garlic, a bass guitar joins as the garlic is tossed into a pan and drizzled with olive oil, then Celenza adds broccoli and piano joins the jazzy composition. One year following the *Frankie Cooks* debut, Celenza recruited his Juilliard-educated brother to help custom compose and record music for the recipes.

The Celenza brothers filmed, produced, and published the show entirely on their own. The show was theirs and when awarded New York Emmy® Awards in 2013, 2014, and 2015 it celebrated *their* creativity and execution. It grew from

---

54   Celenza, Frankie. 2018. "Frankie Celenza". *Tisch.Nyu.Edu*. https:// tisch.nyu.edu/clive-davis-institute/alumni/frankiecelenza.

Frankie's passions and creative abilities into the precise show he imagined with neither need for nor interference of contract and manager because YouTube required none.

"Our mission is to give everyone a voice and show them the world," YouTube's 'About' page reads "upload original content, and share it all with friends, family and the world," its description instructs.[55] The YouTube user, as holds true for other social media platforms, can act independently, produce content cheaply, and spread content broadly. The world could tune into the voice Celenza created on YouTube, and the Emmys® *Frankie Cooks* came to win in 2013 and 2014 confirm an enormous audience. Through social media, Celenza had found a voice and connected with the world, though at its start, Celenza addressed a more defined viewership:

"My audience is my age and younger," Celenza says. "Look, the digital sphere is how you," referring to myself and peers, "communicate with the world."

The media which existed before *Frankie Cooks,* spoke to homeowners and television owners, those in control of the remote. Where the Food Network TV channel attracted an audience akin to my own father, *Frankie Cooks* and other streamed series attracted me.

---

55   "About YouTube". 2018. *Youtube.Com.* https://www.youtube.com/yt/about/.

A Pew Research Center report states that about six in ten of young American adults primarily use online streaming over traditional television.[56] With *Frankie Cooks* Celenza injected food entertainment into this digital entertainment sphere where no remote mattered, and college-aged Frankie, his peers, and the rising generation looked.

At present, Frankie hosts a local televised alongside *Frankie Cooks*, but his digital career has grown tremendously. The *Frankie Cooks* YouTube Page boasts 30,000 subscribers and includes series like "Struggle Meals" to show viewers how to eat well for $2 or less per plate, 'Frankie's World" which melds instruction with a theatrical narrative of a dish's history. Celenza's following also includes his Facebook page (10,783 followers) the Frankie's World Facebook page (117,000 followers) The Struggle Meals Facebook page (540,000 followers), Instagram page (39,900 followers), and the 30 million people following *Tastemade*, the online food and entertainment network for which he now works.

Celenza filled the space between cooks who watched television and those who did not. Though television will not die at the hands of streaming video as soon as tomorrow, the

---

56 "61% Of Young Adults In U.S. Watch Mainly Streaming TV". 2018. *Pew Research Center*. http://www.pewresearch.org/fact-tank/2017/09/13/about-6-in-10-young-adults-in-u-s-primarily-use-online-streaming-to-watch-tv/.

'gap' Celenza sought to fill with his digital series appears to have been more of a forward-thinking abyss, usurping traditional entertainment means to establish a new master on our attentions: streamed video and social media.

His career now spread across both his and *Tastemade's* social media accounts, Celenza finds himself "more inclined to Instagram" where another element of access appears on the side for the viewer.

Any Instagram user finds him or herself in direct connect to people and accounts they follow. If Selena Gomez posts a photo, anyone of her 142 million followers moved to interact with it enjoy the intimate thrill of knowing Selena herself may see their name amongst the thousands of other liked or read and respond to their comment. Here, Celenza interacts immediately with his international fan-base, conversing with them, reading, and responding to their reactions on hour-old posts.

The entirety of Celenza's career developed by transforming the Food Network model of food entertainment for a world driven by digital access, he turned into a new manifestation of media catered for the individual creator eager to connect to the world. He appealed to upcoming audiences using their channels and stayed true to the 'social' facet of social media. His is a story of a heralded change well regarded—access perceived and applied.

CHAPTER 5

NEW VOICES AND FLAVORS

———

"'I wish you to go and dine,' said the Editor-in-Chief to me in September last, 'I wish you to go and dine....Dine somewhere else to-day and somewhere else to-morrow. I wish you to dine everywhere,- from the Astor House Restaurant to the smallest description of dining saloon in the City, in order that you may furnish an account of all these places. The cashier will pay your expense."

— "HOW WE DINE," *THE NEW YORK TIMES* 1859[57]

———

57 The New York Times. 1859. "How We Dine", Anony-
    mous, 1859. https://timesmachine.nytimes.com/timesma-
    chine/1859/01/01/78882285.pdf.

Before the Internet, there was print. Newspapers tossed on doorsteps or sold street-side kept the world up to date on everything including local restaurants in a manner not dissimilar to the 160-year-old example set in the quote above: An anonymous reporter circling about a city, dining, documenting, and disseminating his or her reviews. Publications like *The New York Times* continue the tradition of food criticism, awarding stars and praise as a discerning palette and sharp tongue allow. Though no longer entirely anonymous and wandering deep into neighborhood joints, restaurant reviews maintain their making-and-breaking power.

Yet, in the age of *Yelp* and crowd-sourced ratings, many food journalists have moved on. Though continue to visit restaurant and document the experience, others use the internet's wealth of reviews as greater reason to turn their journalistic attention elsewhere.

* * *

Eggshell colored walls, plush grey cushions, floor to ceiling windows with a view of Louis Vuitton across D.C.'s upscale City Center Plaza. A menu listing entrees in prices ranging from $30 to $50 and toting ingredients fresh from nearby farms rests between chestnut leather folds. Diners sit the table expecting a delightful meal, as the attentive waitstaff, upscale neighborhood and "$$" price would suggest. However, in the winter of 2015, Fig & Olive patrons across the country found themselves, not so satisfied as sick—salmonella sick.

When the salmonella reports surfaced, Jessica Sidman was Food Editor of the *Washington City Paper* and a contributor for its "Young & Hungry" column. As Editor, she did not vow to remain an anonymous critic, but decades of food writers before her had assumed false names, donned disguises, and paid with credit cards for generations. At the *Washington Post* for example, acclaimed food critic and author, Tom Sietsema, cannot recall a time an attempt at anonymity was not a feature of food critic doctrines.[58]

In an interview with *Eater DC* after announcements of Sidman's hire and transparency, *City Paper's* editor, Michael Schaffer confirmed Sidman would break this: "Her title is editor and I want her to write compelling, memorable journalism about food. Jess gave us a very strong pitch to do a different kind of food journalism."[59] The food reporting Sidman pursued, broke the veil of restaurant reviewer, and

---

58 Carman, Tim. 2012. "New Young & Hungry Columnist Anonymous". *Washington Post.* https://www.washingtonpost.com/blogs/all-we-can-eat/post/new-young-and-hungry-columnist-wont-be-anonymous/2012/05/02/gIQArXaJxT_blog.html?utm_term=.f5c27f744e37&wprss=rss_all-we-can-eat.

59 McKeever, Amy. 2018. "City Paper Editor Michael Schaffer On Critics & Anonymity". *Eater DC.* https://dc.eater.com/2012/5/3/6590261/city-paper-editor-michael-schaffer-on-critics-anonymity.

fought to shatter the two dimensions into which most readers grouped food writing: criticism or recipes.

She envisioned fulfilling "actual reporting" impulses in the culinary arts, an attempt to "cover food as culture and politics and art." "A lot of times," Sidman explains, "there is a really low bar for food writers, but there is no reason for a food reporter not to be an investigator." Sidman craved what Schaffer referred to as "shoe-leather journalism," dogged, investigative, and interactive. When word rose of Fig & Olive's link to the salmonella outbreak, Sidman went to work.

Sidman did not break the salmonella story, but wanted to document the long-term impact Fig & Olive's temporarily shut down would yield on the business. She pulled documents, interviewed victims suffering the aliments of salmonella, and analyzed the Department of Health's report of Fig & Olive. Her investigation led her to file a Freedom of Information Act request, or FOIA, from the health department.

A FOIA requests information from government agencies for information. Responding to her request, Sidman received a mass of emails between restaurants and the health department, which included documentation on how Fig & Olive prepared their meals. Information that Fig & Olive's food was, in truth, not at all what its ambiance, prices and menu promised. The first line of her published article reads as follows:

"When you order truffle risotto at an upscale restaurant—the kind that lists local farms at the top of its menu—you might expect that the dish is prepared fresh, from-scratch in the kitchen. But at **Fig & Olive**, the $26 truffle risotto (no longer on the menu) was pre-cooked and frozen at a central commissary in Long Island City, New York, then shipped to restaurants around the country, where it was reheated with cheese and garnished."[60]

Beneath a series of pictures demonstrating how the above mentioned truffle risotto was to be measured, covered in parmesan, reheated, tossed with scallions, and aesthetically arranged on a warmed plate. Sidman continues on to explain that "nearly 220 dish components, including soups, sauces, purees, dressings, desserts, breads, ratatouille, ravioli, crab cakes, pre-cooked chicken tagine, pre-cooked paella, and more." She even revealed the restaurant's truffle oil aioli was made with not raw or pasteurized egg as a traditional recipe calls, but Hellmann's mayonnaise.

Since the Fig & Olive article, Sidman continues to write stories that push the boundaries of stereotypically defined food writing. In a world of *Yelp* reviews, "everyone has an opinion,

---

60 Sidman, Jessica. 2015. "Investigation Reveals Fig & Olive's Kitchen Relics On Pre-Made Meal Components". *Washington City Paper.* https://www.washingtoncitypaper.com/food/blog/20678796/investigation-finds-fig-olives-kitchen-relies-on-pre-made-meal-components.

everyone is a foodie, less and less do you need a critic for that," Sidman explains, "you can't just throw out an opinion." The rise of social media and online communities grants individuals a voice with the instantaneous power to vote, rate, critique, or compliment dining experiences. In this crowded space, food journalists must carve for themselves a unique voice, authority, and perspective. Even the best reviews by the country's top critics, are "very little about 'salty' or 'service,'" she continues, these reviews are "taking on a cultural topic, a personality." Fig & Olive never apologized, but Sidman's article created a PR nightmare for the company, and with it, Sidman staked a new role and power for food writing.

Sidman is not alone in her pursuit of broadened food writing. As Sidman's story demonstrates, the genesis of the Food Internet brings users into contact with far more than pretty plates and over-the-table brunch photos. Entire platforms have sprung up around the goal of bringing visitors into full contact with the food world.

"The way that we think about food has really changed in the past few years," Sonia Chopra, Managing Editor for *Eater*, begins, "we get to take a deep close look at how businesses operate and how people in power exhibit that power." At first take, one might not associate this description of food media and the content a food and travel publisher like *Eater* disseminates but this is Sonia's point precisely.

"Three years ago, people were quick to say something funny for a reaction," but things shifted and Chopra, along with much of the food media industry feels a push toward "more sensitivity to the sincere, the purpose driven." The development of the Food Internet pushes not simply the food related media but the way we think about food. The attention the mere topic of food receives inevitably places a new premium on food as cultural currency, reassigning the value food culture places on a dish or cuisine, redefining what exactly food means to our cities, states, and, according to Chopra, national identity and politics.

The Food Internet, as Chopra claims "democratizes everything" and in terms of food media "people have access [to] information that people haven't seen before." With access like never before, the information, tensions, politics, and power structures touching all corners of the culinary world can be thrust into the light, flipped over and journalists may declare their findings from the mount of a publishing platform, like *Eater*, that claims a readership numbering in the thousands. These culinary exposés often begin with a single question "If a political decision is made, how does that influence the food and restaurant scene?"

Sonia's first example? The #MeToo movement.

The #MeToo movement brought to the social media spotlight the prevalence of sexual harassment. A digitally native movement, the hash tag (#MeToo) concluded account after account of, typically, workplace sexual harassment, raising a sea of online voices united in their similar experiences and discomforts. With the hashtag, victims' broke their silence, and included the hashtag to symbolize yet another member to the army of individuals no longer content with silent suffering. The #MeToo campaign and the broader change the movement symbolized for workplace environments seeped into the culinary scene.

"If you were harassed in a restaurant and didn't know how to handle it, now you know there's a platform for that," Sonia explained. A desperately needed platform at that. According to data from the Equal Employment Opportunity Commission, more sexual harassment claims are filed from restaurants than from any other industry; over 10,000 employees in full-service restaurants filed sexual harassment claims between 1990 and 2016.[61] The digital world surrounding food empowers voices. In December of 2017, *Bon Appetite* published an article summarizing the names and sexual harassment allegations against at least four public figures

61 Vo, Lam Thuy. 2017. "We Got Government Data On 20 Years Of Workplace Sexual Harassment Claims. These Charts Break It Down.". *Buzzfeednews.Com*. https://www.buzzfeednews.com/article/lamvo/eeoc-sexual-harassment-data#.svGEBJPrVV.

in the restaurant business including Ken Friedman, Mario Batali, Johnny Iuzzini, and John Besh. In early 2018, Chef Mike Isabella was also accused of sexual misconduct in the work place.[62]

At the time of writing, Isabella has not confessed to any of the allegations regarding his behavior. Chopra and the *Eater* staff saw the allegation alone as a cause for action. Mike Isabella operates eleven restaurants in the D.C. metropolitan area, many of which have been recognized with awards, and Isabella himself has appeared on popular television culinary shows including *Top Chef.* But these achievements and the award winning quality of his establishments' food amount to nothing in the face of sexual misconduct allegations, in *Eater's* eyes. With no tolerance for allegations, *Eater* pulled Mike Isabella's restaurants from their interactive maps in a clear demonstration of disapproval. Moreover, *Eater* is not alone in its protest.

The James Beard Foundation is an American culinary foundation established in 1990 that presents annual awards to honor a wide range of food professions for excellence in cuisine, culinary writing, and culinary education. This

---

62   Rojas, Warren. 2018. "Isabella Eatery Manager Sues Mike Isabella For Sexual Harassment [Updated]". *Eater DC.* https://dc.eater.com/2018/3/19/17139870/ mike-isabella-chloe-caras-sexual-harassment.

year, the Foundation included a new standard of excellence, behavior. As of early 2018, the Foundation's values include the following:

"The foundation is guided by the values of respect, transparency, diversity, sustainability, and equality. We believe that in order to achieve our mission, it is expected that everyone who works in and with the foundation shares similar values and operates with integrity."[63]

The Internet as a platform empowers voices to incite change, and the Food Internet is by no means excluded, inspiring real change and impactful action across the entire culinary industry. As Sonia puts it, "Everyone is keenly aware that we stand by everything we do… everyone on the Internet is aware of how long things exist on the Internet, we have a responsibility to tell true stories and stories that matter." These stories, the ones that 'matter' span far beyond food porn, but Chopra and her team understand food to mean far more than cheese pulls, microwave mug cakes, and waffled tatertots.

"Why are you talking about politics, you're supposed to just be food?" This is the kind of protest Chopra and other food

---

63 Severson, Kim. 2018. "James Beard Awards Apply A New Yardstick: Good Behavior". *Nytimes.Com*. https://www.nytimes.com/2018/02/15/dining/james-beard-awards-sexual-harassment.html.

media publishers hear, but she stands firmly by a belief that "food is culture, food is politics" and it is her job as a publisher to take food seriously on that front. So when a cultural food tops news feeds and fills Instagram pages everywhere, it is Chopra and *Eater's* job to provide context. Take kakigori for example.

Kakigori is a shaved-ice specialty dessert with a history in traditional Japanese cuisine going back to the dining delicacies of 11th century Japanese elites.[64] Given the dessert is gaining quick popularity across the U.S., Chopra's team at *Eater* set out to investigate one of New York's most popular kakigori spots and shoot a story. When they returned, Chopra didn't meet an enthusiastic team, full of kakigori and excited to bring their find to the millions of *Eater's* readers. Rather, Chopra's team was hesitant, neither confident nor comfortable with the story. Why? Because the kakigori they found was served not with an understanding of the tradition of the dish within Japanese culture, how the dish was only made available to the public in the late 19th century when ice too became accessible to the common man. Rather, the shop was opened with an understanding of just how much New York's food scene would love the treat and how much guests would be willing to pay for a serving.

64   Krishna, Priya. 2018. "Why An Ancient Frozen Japanese Specialty Is America'S Hottest Dessert". *Grub Street*. http://www.grubstreet. com/2018/03/kakigori-pastry-chefs.html.

For Chopra and her team, food is more than a cute Instagram. No dish comes without a background, and every kitchen and table is an opportunity to unearth, investigate, and challenge the politics at hand. At a time when national authorities express an obvious and clear distaste for media, when a majority of Americans feel a rising degree of disease toward and distrust of media and politics, with one Gallup poll claiming only 32% of Americans have a "great deal or fair amount of trust in the media."[65] When minorities and the multitude of cultures comprising the American identity are finding spotlights and voices of their own, the food media industry might just be the voice America needs.

Publishers like *Eater* and the *Washingtonian* swing wide open the doors of restaurant kitchens and pull back the curtains shrouding elite tables to give readers the entire story of the food on their plates. Food is not an isolated entity—politics, national culture, and corporate values affect who eats what and where he or she eats it. These and similar publishers do not treat it as such, they create media to this end, giving its audiences the truest taste of their food. Branded as an authority dedicated to food truths and objective reporting, they earn loyal, growing followings, preserving the food-reporting world as a branch of the media worthy of public trust.

---

65 Swift, Art. 2018. "Americans' Trust In Mass Media Sinks To New Low". *Gallup.Com*. https://news.gallup.com/poll/195542/americans-trust-mass-media-sinks-new-low.aspx.

PART III

CONNECT

"Food is the great connector"

—*PHIL ROSENTHAL*[66]

The world is not always a happy place.

Floods and mud drowned cities in Japan, volcanoes covered the tropics of Guatemala and Hawaii in black ash and molten lava; political turmoil sent thousands to the streets in angry disquietude, the United States saw about one school shooting per week through May and all the while death tolls click

---

66 Serious Eats. 2018. "Phil Rosenthal Is Anthony Bourdain Except Afraid Of Everything". Podcast. *Serious Eats.*

higher and higher in places like Syria, Yemen, Iraq, Afghanistan, and Mexico—to name a few.[67] As I write, we've only just passed the year's halfway mile marker. No, there is not a period of history remiss of tragedy's ugly scar. But in our interconnected digital age, the whole of mankind sees it all, hears it all, and together holds his or her breath waiting for the next shoe to drop.

In this state, where each morning's news hour brings freshly collected updates on what may appear to be the world's demise, is it of any real shock many of us have turned inward to our home's kitchens and local restaurant tables where colorful plates await with the warm promise of nourishment, flavor, and if nothing else, full bellies? When global tragedy strikes, the *New York Times*' recipe archives see an immediate spike in visitors—perhaps reaffirmation of the biological link between stress and eating or perhaps a commentary on the communal forces of comfort in food found when gathered as one of many round a table.[68]

Cesar Chavez famously said, "If you really want to make friends, go to someone's house and eat with him - the people

67 Walker, Christina, and Saeed Ahmed. 2018. "There Has Been, On Average, 1 School Shooting Every Week This Year". *CNN*. https://www.cnn.com/2018/03/02/us/school-shootings-2018-list-trnd/index.html.

68 "Why Stress Causes People To Overeat - Harvard Health". 2018. *Harvard Health*. https://www.health.harvard.edu/newsletter_article/why-stress-causes-people-to-overeat.

who give you their food, give you their heart." We find in pausing our day to focus on our plates and company greater space to connect and time to grow together. We cannot sit down to table with others and find ourselves entirely alone.

Digital apparitions of food do not diverge from these communal impulses. Rather, they appear most frequently in the internet's 'social' sectors. Facebook, Instagram, Snapchat, YouTube and Reddit circulate food media on a daily basis. Entire communities develop around food online, recipes are shared, and conversations spring forth about a dish, or at least, a picture of one.

The best of food media appreciates food as a binding agent, acknowledging it as a coping method much needed in a time when everyone knows nearly every terrible thing. It does not degrade food's digital manifestations, writing the associated mass 'foodie' movement off as an imposter population too heavily attached to their Instagrams. No, in many ways the serial avocado toast 'grammer and newspaper food critic are not comparable, but they share a species and benefit from the same base comfort their grub provides despite their differing expressions. The best of digital food media holds food in highest esteem by seeing in the digital, greater opportunity to bring people together around a dish.

CHAPTER 6

MAKING IT PERSONAL

———

Self-described as a "newspaper man," Sifton contributed to the *The Times* under the title of "editor" for a varied collection of sections, serving as National Editor and Culture Editor before accepting his current position as the Editor of the Food section.

"A newspaper man" is what Sam Sifton, Editor of *The New York Times* Food and Cooking section, describes himself as. "Newspaper man," a descriptor whose inclusionary nature joins Sifton's professional past and present. It lumps together what he did and did not write regarding food, capturing the whole of his career. From his success in each editorial position we could learn a great deal about storytelling, criticism or the best way of catching and keeping readers' attention. However, what may be richest, as is so often the case with good stories, are the points of tension—the falls and fails and lessons learned along the way which ultimately reveal more than the perfect pleasantness of smooth sailing.

While writing for the national desk, Sifton's writing took the authoritative shape of informational. His job was to relay the *news*, updating millions of *Times* readers with the degree of factual authority expected of the press. The personal had little place here so the third person voice, the objective voice, dominated Sifton's work. "He," "she," "they," "it"—the man behind the writing barely visible, fading behind the 'he,' 'she' and 'theys' subject matter. But Sifton's transition into Culture and Arts sections of the *Times* requested the personal perspective come forward to reflect, comment, and criticize.

As food critic, he had no choice but to root his writing in personal experience. His colorful reviews included zinger lines which described "a Milanese-style veal cutlet," as "essentially a breaded and fried laptop case, [served] with lemon, arugula, ricotta salata and a garish, oily salsa verde."[69] He concludes one review with one side note on the dish, "(Credit where it's due: It came out this way twice, a month apart)."[70] But even here, the vulnerable singularity of "I" could be avoided.

---

69   Sifton, Sam. 2010. "Kenmare". *The New York Times | Food*, , 2010. https://www.nytimes.com/2010/07/07/dining/reviews/07rest. html?ref=samsifton.

70   Ibid.

Prior to *New York Times Food* and *Cooking,* Sifton claims he "never" used the first person. Four years into his role as Editor, Sifton was still fighting hard against it. He experimented with the first person plural, "we," yet this was "faux idiosyncratic," as Sifton describes; a bitter falsehood readers would undoubtedly pick up. In this role, Sifton also built the enormous recipe archive of *NYT Cooking.* Slowly, his reluctance melted in the face of pragmaticism, sincerity, and a necessary newsletter for *NYT Cooking.*

The Newsletter, a letter from Sifton, arrives in over 1 million inboxes prompts readers to visit the *NYT Cooking* archives to follow the letter's suggestions on "What to cook this week" or discover recipes of their own choosing. The letter sent on August 29, titled "Cooking: What I Did on My Summer Vacation" reads as follows:

"Good morning. You miss me? I spent the last two weeks up in Maine, chopping on a wood stove, chasing fish and reading books. I didn't cook with recipes. I just cooked: chunks of goat simmered with mango chutney, rice wine, soy sauce and red-pepper sauce; ground beef chili with peanut butter and smoked paprika; canned duck confit with duck-fat roasted potatoes; roasted cauliflower in a cheese sauce I thinned out with beer. (Go Badgers!) I griddled a lot of sausages. I composed a lot of salads. I baked a lot of bread.

"By far the best thing I came up with was a childishly simple lamb stew. The meat came from Apple Creek Farm in Bowdoinham, and I did almost nothing to it. Just put down a layer of sliced onions in a Dutch oven, followed by cubed potatoes and carrots, followed by the lamb. Added salt, pepper, some water so that the meat took on the appearance of the rocks and ledges at half tide in the bay outside. I slid that into the oven and let it cook for a whole bunch of hours next to a dying fire...

"Someday soon you should try that, if you can get some small-farm, well-educated, poetry-reading, $18-a-pound lamb at your farmer's market, some root vegetables to match. You will not be sorry."[71]

"I" defines the newsletter, giving what is still a marketing tactic the semblance of a true letter. The recounted recipes, the reflection of the bay in the stew, and the picture of poetry-reading lamb are Sifton's own. Far from the third-person impersonal, the letter is personal.

* * *

Sami Main worked for *AdWeek*, more specifically, she was *AdWeek's* digital media reporter meaning hundreds of

---

71   Sifton, Sam. Letter Anabelle Nuelle to. 2018. "Cooking: What I Did On My Summer Vacation". Email, 2018.

articles, examples and pages whizz by her eyes each day as she writes, edits and keeps a wary eye on what advertising happened on social media. In her words, Main "looks for creative ways to communicate what's new" —- because social media is exactly where "what's new" gets communicated.

The Pew Research Center reported in August of 2017 that two-thirds of Americans (roughly 67%) get at least part of their news on social media.[72] No longer is Facebook a simple means of connection, best leveraged to see past roommates' wedding and baby photos. As the significance of platforms such as Facebook, Instagram, Snapchat, and Twitter continues to grow, so does their influence—and advertisers and publishers have taken note.

So, Main doesn't just write about who Tweeted what, and which Facebook videos happen to be trending. She writes and reviews articles covering what advertisers are doing with social media's vast powers. To *AdWeek's* own social media pages, she posts articles like "The True Story Behind These Delightfully Infuriating Ads in New York City's Subway Cars" or a list of "The 22 Most Engaging Pieces of Branded Content on Social Media in 2017." Also included in her repertoire: the food corner of the internet, its brands, its publishers, and its communities. This is where I found Main.

---

72 *Research Center's Journalism Project.* http://www.journalism.
    org/2017/09/07/news-use-across-social-media-platforms-2017/.

"Why Genius Kitchen Servers Up Relatable Food Content to Millennials: 56% of young Americans want to improve their cooking skills"[73]

"How Condé Nast's Food Innovation Group Plans to Take Over the 'Food Internet'"[74]

"Food52 and the Unique Space it Occupies on the Food Internet: Connects content with contributors and brands, plus its own products"[75]

These articles were my first interaction with Main's expertise in food's online presence. From her, I learned how Condé Nast capitalized on the growing demand for food content by packaging the branches of its digital food content—including the *Bon Appétit* magazine and the accompanying digital platforms, the popular recipe website and app *Epicurious*, and Condé Nast's own network of blog influencers and branded content—under a single entity, the Food Innovation Group,

---

73 Main, Sami. 2018. "Why Genius Kitchen Serves Up Relatable Food Content To Millennials". *Adweek.Com*. https://www.adweek.com/creativity/why-genius-kitchen-serves-up-relatable-food-content-to-millennials/.

74 Main, Sami. 2018. "How Condé Nast's Food Innovation Group Plans To Take Over The 'Food Internet'". *Adweek.Com*. https://www.adweek.com/digital/how-cond-nasts-food-innovation-group-plans-take-over-food-internet-175101/.

75 Main, Sami. 2018. "Food52 And The Unique Space It Occupies On The Food Internet". *Adweek.Com*. https://www.adweek.com/digital/food52-and-the-unique-space-it-occupies-on-the-food-internet/.

to 'own' the food internet and effectively offer advertisers a streamlined entry into all corners of the digital food world.[76] As a self-professed consumer of digital food content and with a professional finger on the pulse of the digital trends and an eye on exactly what kind of content dominates each corner of social media, Sami Main knows the Food Internet. So when I spoke to her over the phone, we began our conversation from the beginning, the birth of the Food Internet.

Main opens the story with the rise of the personal blog. Here, home baked cookies are photographed in bright natural lighting with white and pastel backgrounds. The photos divide a narrative about the day surrounding the making of the cookies and in the last of which, the original bountiful collection of perfectly round chocolate chip cookies clearly diminishes to only a few.

These are the "essay then recipe" blogs, Main jokes, laughing about scrolling through what might feel like an eternity of personal narrative to a reader anxiously searching for the ingredient list. These are the stories, recipes and pages that that filled and inspired the Pinterest community. And for this sect of the Food Internet, in Main's eyes, the word "community" deserves a special underline. For the beginning of

---

76   Food Innovation Group. 2018. "Home - Food Innovation Group". *Foodinnovationgroup.Com*. http://www.foodinnovationgroup. com/.

the food internet was more than content, it was "useful and precious, and still genuine"; it was a community through and through.

Fast forward five to seven years and the contemporary Food Internet arrives. No longer for the home cook recounting personal anecdotes alongside cooking or baking mishaps alone, the Food Internet became increasingly commercial, a place for brands and serious profit. Food and beverage, culinary and lifestyle publishers increasingly populated the digital sphere. The food internet, full of pictures of bright dishes captured in low natural light against dark wood backgrounds, was everywhere. Publishers spat out content, and individual voices merged into the buzz of hundreds of others, engulfed by a sea of florescent smoothie bowls and abounding milkshakes.

I paused Main here at this content tipping point. Her interest in this digital sector emanated from a personal past time but with her description of the Food Internet's commercial turning point, a professional tone entered her voice.

"So are you a loyal follower to anyone?" I ventured. "Yes and no…as social media editor, everything flies by" Main began, listing off the publishers and personalities she personally follows and her reasoning for each:

- Johnny Sun, the Canadian humorist and author of "everyone's a aliebn when ur a aliebn too," the illustrated book who frequently posts stories of his cooking. Why does Main watch these stories? Because "it's first person in a way," cooks food he likes, he plays music in the background, and mentions his friends in the stories.
- Food52, the culinary publisher and online community with a reputation for beautiful food photographs. Main's motivation: The posts are "personable without wasting your time."
- Molly Yeh, the well known author of cookbook-memoir *Molly On the Range: Recipes and Stories from an Unlikely Life on the Farm,* food blogger and Julliard-trained percussionist who now stars in Food Network's new series, *Girl Meets Farm.* Main follows Yeh because "she's just telling you stories, its personal."

"Person," "personable," "personal"—these are Main's reasons. Sun shows himself as a whole person with friends, a certain taste in music, and culinary palate; Food52 infuses its posts with a 'personable' warmth, while Yeh's life and background govern her cooking, not the other way around.

Authentic voices distinguish these accounts. When she chooses to read or watch a post, she chooses based their quirks, humor, the real details of their everyday. She seeks the same sincerity from branded content. She trusts the person behind the content, the familiar voice walking her through a recipe or an article, happiest when the face on the screen is familiar.

For food in particular, what cements her loyalty is the individual whose presence offers opportunity for connection. An episode from NPR's Hidden Braid explores the bond between people and food, particularly when they "break bread together."[77] Social science correspondent, Shankar Vedantam, explained findings by Ayelet Fishback of the University of Chicago which suggested eating the same dish as another person increasing the amount of trust and cooperation felt between the two parties. "Food is about bringing something into the body," Fishbach begins, "And to eat the same food suggests that we are both willing to bring the same thing into our bodies. People just feel closer to people who are eating the same food as they do. And then trust, cooperation, these are just consequences of feeling close to someone."[78] Main, a connoisseur of content, seeks "I" in food media.

* * *

When describing his newsletters, Sifton claims his readers "tolerate [his] interests." Inevitably, these interests appear in

---

77   NPR. 2017. "Why Eating The Same Food Increases People's Trust And Cooperation". Podcast. *Morning Edition*. https://www.npr.org/2017/02/02/512998465/why-eating-the-same-food-increases-peoples-trust-and-cooperation.

78   Ibid.

every letter, because Sifton uses the first person—his newsletter "takes time, acknowledges that yesterday was a shitty day, or there was a terror attack in Paris." The letter is "rooted in reality, then it makes an argument, an argument that I [Sifton] passionately believe that if you make food with others, your life would be better."

Sifton offers his interests and experiences, with the simple hope some portion of the millions of subscribers might resonate with the content but he writes with neither intent nor expectation of crowd-pleasing. "What to Cook This Week" arrives in the inbox, addressing the same world and shared experiences of its recipients, and suggests responding to the day with a shared meal tonight.

.

CHAPTER 7

"INSTAGRAM, A COMMUNITY OF OVER 1 BILLION..."[79]

Communities have leaders, guides, governors, and in the digital community of Instagram, we call them 'influencers'.

An "influencer" in the business world, according to the Cambridge Dictionary, is "a person or group that has the ability to influence the behavior or opinions of others."[80] According to an article by *Food & Wine*, which polled some of the most

---

79 "About Us • Instagram". 2018. *Instagram.Com.* https://www.instagram.com/about/us/.
80 "Influencer". 2018. *Cambridge Dictionary.* Cambridge University Press. https://dictionary.cambridge.org/us/dictionary/english/influencer.

beloved food accounts on Instagram, one need only follow five simple steps to become an Instagram influencer:[81]

1. "Pick a Catchy Name"
According to the Instagram influencer behind the @food account followed by over 544,000 others, Sarah Phillips, the name has to be "an easy-to-remember name or one that easily explains who you are"

2. "Know Your Brand"
As Alexa Mehraban of @eatingNYC explains Instagram success hinges on claiming a specific purpose to be heard amongst the thousands of food-centric accounts.

3. "Take a Photography Class"
If you intend to build an audience and an income around your content on a visual platform, your content has to be worth following. Still, Mehraban ranks posting every day, even with "so-so pictures," better than infrequently posting the best shots—it's not just content, its relevancy.

4. "Make Friends"
What is a social network without a network after all? This was the secret to The Modern Proper's Instagram

---

81 Kramer, Jillian. 2018. "How to Become a Food Instagram Influencer". *Food & Wine*. https://www.foodandwine.com/how-to-be-food-influencer.

account—finding similar accounts and building real relationships with each via a dance of tagging, commenting, direct messaging and eventually coordinated travel.

5. "Consider that You May Have to Work for Less"
Crowdedness in the Instagram influencer world has driven down the price of influencing. With more and more people ready to post for free, the checks from brands have become smaller and smaller, or disappeared in place of merchandise exchanges. This being said, Chelsea Naftelberg of the Attention social media agency still began influencer negotiations at $1,000 per 100,000 followers in late 2017.[82]

A stream of saturated and polished images and perfectly captured photoFor marketing purposes, an influencer is an asset, a trusted endorser able of broadcasting a product endorsement to hundreds and thousands of people, but an influencer at the end of the day, is a person. And for this reason, Tucker Iida, the man behind @explorewithtaka and founder of LA's Takasan, would place a special premium on 4. "Make Friends."

A graduate of Cornell's School of Hotel Administration, Iida pointed his education toward a career in crux of business and

82   Chen, Yuyu. 2017. "What Influencer Marketing Really Costs". *Digiday*. https://digiday.com/marketing/what-influencer-marketing-costs/.

pleasure. He knew what he wanted—a brick and mortar, fast casual restaurant inspired by the food he grew up with in Tokyo—but a direct leap from graduation to opening doors felt too rash. He wanted time, resources and an unshakable foothold in the culinary scene. So when his time at Cornell came to a close, Iida moved to Los Angeles, found a job and made an Instagram.

L.A. is consistently ranked among the top food cities in America and even the world, so Iida needed more than his first job at Tasty and later *Tastemade* to find his place there.[83] He needed a platform. When he first moved out to L.A. Instagram was "never business, always personal," yet Instagram to a food city is a near rite of passage. Slowly, Iida began to join L.A.'s Instagram communitiy.

"I started small, started liking people's pages, then adding hashtags, and commenting," before upgrading to "tagging people in images" and finally "[he] started reaching out, direct messaging people." As he filled his Instagram with photos of the food he ate and the places he visited while bouncing between Los Angeles, New York, and Tokyo, he continued tagging, hash tagging, and direct messaging. @

---

83 Ferguson, Gillian. 2017. "How Los Angeles Became One
     of the Best Food Cities in the World". *Food & Wine*.
     https://www.foodandwine.com/travel/restaurants/
     best-food-cities-2017-los-angeles.

explorewithtaka's follower ticker climbed: 1,000, 5,000, 10,000, 12,000 and kept going. "Little by little I reached out to influencers" and before long he'd see them at the events to which only top food influencers are invited.

The above outlined steps to becoming an Instagram influencer gloss over these events entirely. A restaurant will host a media event in the hopes of getting more social media attention to promote their business, inviting and paying an influencer, the "host" so to speak, who in turn invites his or her influencer friends. Typically, restaurants let the attendees order whatever they want from the menu to be photographed and enjoyed though sometimes sit restaurants will present a pre-selected spread of food to be photographed, only after which are the attendees invited to order and dine. Either way, influencers enjoy a free meal in exchange for an appetizing posted photo.

Thus a photo appears to be worth, at least a free meal, but not all of the photographers posting photos of food enjoy the luxury of a complimentary meal. A photo is not worth a free meal, but a following is.

"Everyone who does Insta understands the community," Iida continues, relationship building powers social media success. As Iida explains, the higher the following, the higher the credibility, more credibility means more opportunities which in turn brings more friends. The circle grows and the cycle repeats, cranking the lever behind every 10K+ follower-strong account.

The premium on relationships supports the rise of Popular-Pays, a startup whose platform enables easy connection and collaboration between creators and companies, and influencer marketing on the whole.[84] In an interview, PopularPays CEO and Founder, Corbett Drummey, notes "The most highly-rated posts tend to be authentic and creative. In studies we've conducted on Facebook ads, our content outperformed our sources in brand awareness and recall."[85] Why? Because authentic content bearing the mark of a unique mark of an individual answering, in turn, a human impulse for sincere connection.

The fashion world too has an irrefutable fleet of influencers. People like Chiara Ferragni, founder of @theblondesalad Instagram account, who started as a law student in Milan documenting her outfits now has 612 thousand followers and wore wedding gowns that were custom made by Dior in her recent marriage to Italian musician, Fedez. A 2015 Harvard

84 "Popular Pays: Create Content Worth Sharing". 2018. *Popular Pays*. https://www.popularpays.com/.

85 Cooke, Jayna. 2018. "Is It Worth Sharing? Corbett Drummey And The Question That Built Popular Pays". *Forbes*. https://www.forbes.com/sites/jaynacooke/2018/01/12/is-it-worth-sharing-corbett-drummey-and-the-question-that-built-popular-pays/#5c1108d5356f.

Business School case study estimated Ferragni had generated close to $10 million in revenue, charging brands to appear at events or endorse products alongside the glimpses into her life.[86] Famous for being themselves there is an assumed quality of realness, felt in connecting to an individual. Unlike fashion, the innate communal aspect of the food gives its influencers a leg up.

In the Spring of 2017, research by R.I.M. Dunbar of the University of Oxford's Experimental Psychology department found a tie between social eating and happiness. The study found sharing meals with family or friends provides "social and individual benefits," noting that "those who eat socially more often feel happier and are more satisfied with life, are more trusting of others, are more engaged with their local communities, and have more friends they can depend on for support."[87]

Though no research comparing the experience of sharing a meal with that of liking the same food photo, there remains the notion of 'sharing' in both. People like Iida and other influencers serve as the initiators of those bonds. They

86 Larocca, Amy. 2018. "How Influencers Became The New Fashion Establishment". *The Cut*. https://www.thecut.com/2018/02/insta-gram-influencers-are-the-new-fashion-establishment.html.

87 Dunbar, R. I. M. 2017. "Breaking Bread: The Functions Of Social Eating". *Adaptive Human Behavior And Physiology* 3 (3): 198-211. doi:10.1007/s40750-017-0061-4.

prompt solidarity around the dishes they offer via the feeds of their community of followers.

To the brands, restaurants, and entities documented, a post from a popular influencer matches that of a personal recommendation passed on to thousands of others. As Lynn Chen, actor and founder of the food and lifestyle blog *The Actor's Diet,* remarked: "An 'influencer" is expected to be transparent about what it is you're selling… there is an expectation that what you see is real because it's not under the guise of commercial or TV show in the same way." Followers are not following ads (though brands have a place here too), they follow people with accounts.

Thus, online and off, a community is built of people, unique individuals bound together by a shared interest. The "Instagram community" is a community in every right, motivated on all sides by relationship building. The leaders, its influencers, retain their impact by acting, most obviously, as people and, for the Food Internet, eaters.

* * *

In December 2017, less than one year after graduating from Cornell, Takasan opened its doors in downtown L.A.

Takasan is "industrial zen", as Iida describes it. High white walls with touches of greenery against cement, the space mixes the hard precision of utilitarian minimalism and the softness of the natural world.[88] "Ambiance is a huge part of eating... we eat with our eyes," Iida told *L.A. Downtowner*. What diners actually consume at Takasan is donburi, a "Japanese comfort food dish," as its website describes, in which steamed rice is topped with ingredients in sauce dependent upon the region and season.[89] What best compliments the Japanese comfort food and contemporary minimalism of Takasan is the long slab of pale wood running down the center of the space. It is the only table inside Takasan meaning any patrons dining in must sit around it, together. Because in the heart of downtown L.A. eating is about connection and comfort.

Takasan continues to receive its fair share of media attention, even making the *EaterLA* Winter 2018 list of "The Hottest Los Angeles Cheap Eats Restaurants" and earning a visit from one of Iida's own idols, David Chang.[90]

---

88 "Takasan: Bowling For Your Buds". 2017. *LA Downtowner*. https://www.ladowntowner.com/articles/2018/2/takasan.

89 "Takasan". 2018. *Takasan.*. Accessed October 13. https://www.takasan.co/.

90 "The 15 Hottest Los Angeles Cheap Eats Restaurants". 2018. *Eater LA*. https://la.eater.com/maps/best-los-angeles-cheap-eats-affordable-restaurants.

The community from which Iida rose still propels Iida. When @FoodBabyNY, the Instagram account followed by over 304 thousand people featuring photos of delicious food held in front of the account owner's darling children, traveled cross country to L.A., Iida used his pre-existing network to invite the family for donburi.[91] The account posted a single photo of two bowls from Takasan held in front of the account's sleeping star, and accumulated over 3,000 likes. More recently, @ popeyethefoodie, an account starring Popeye the Foodie Dog, an "L.A. stray pup (mix unknown) turned food connoisseur," with over 324 thousand followers also stopped by Takasan.[92] Popeye apparently enjoyed katsu don, a donburi bowl topped with fried chicken, dashi, onion and eggs—and 18,000 people liked Popeye's visit.

---

91   Chau, Mike. 2018. Blog. *@Foodbabyny*. Accessed July 13. https://www.instagram.com/foodbabyny/.

92   2018. Blog. *@Popeyethefoodie*. https://www.instagram.com/p/Bd6cvEEHqbO/?taken-by=popeyethefoodie.

CHAPTER 8

CONNECTION OFFLINE

———

The Northeast and the Deep South of the United States are very different. In one, people buzz by one another, friendly (sometimes) but in a hurry, the winters are cold but the fall is breathtaking. In the other, people move slowly as only one should in the high humid heat of summer, wave to strangers and 'yes' or 'no' never come without a "ma'am" or a "sir." Every now and then, a northerner moves south and finds him or herself in complete transition—training themselves to walk just a few notches slower, appreciate the slow drawl of the new neighbors over the sharp consonants of the North and take no offense when called "ma'am." But what needs no adjustment when a northerner moves South is the food. Gravy, barbecue, fluffy biscuits, and pecan pie, the food of the South defines comfort food. When northerner, Kate

Wood, moved to Lower Alabama, "LA" as Wood calls it, she too found ease in food.

·

For years, Wood dreamed of writing a book, and decided to test the waters by first beginning her own blog. So in 2015, Wood began photographing some of her culinary creations and posting them online. The step was a big one, each time she had considered starting her blog fear blocked the way. "It was 150% fear of man," Wood explains, "What will my friends, and the people in my community say? Will it come off as self-promotion?" But Wood's husband pushed her, and after much praise from friends and family, Kate Wood created *Wood and Spoon*.

"Apple Crisp Ice Cream," Wood and Spoon's first post, begins with a simple photo—a white background lit from the left, interrupted by an ice cream scoop coated by a thin melted layer of caramel colored ice cream.[93] To the scoop's right is the main event: a ceramic ice cream dish filled with the ice cream, topped with pecans. A stuffed ice cream cone rests in the indent the scooper made. No fanfare required—decadent, delicious, and creamy. Theatrics would only spoil the simple goodness of homemade ice cream.

---

93   Wood, Kate. 2018. "Apple Crisp Ice Cream". *Wood & Spoon*. http://
     thewoodandspoon.com/apple-crisp-ice-cream/.

Below the photo, Wood bemoans the end of summer: "How about we all stop with our no white wearing regulations and obligatory drinking of spicy beverages and just agree to agree that summer and fall can combine to make something magical and delicious. At least through September?" Her solution: Apple Crisp Ice Cream, a beautiful concoction of the "Brown Sugar Cream Cheese Ice Cream" by Joy Wilson of "Homemade Decadence," Oatmeal Cookie Crumbs and Apple Crisp Bits.

Cast in grey and light pink, the Wood and Spoon blog is where the by-day clinical dietician "liberally practice[s her] 'everything in moderation' motto by baking and experimenting with new recipes and flavors." The recipe index features only eight categories, six of which are dessert: cakes, pies, frozen desserts, cookies, bread, and candies and confections. Included also, are glimpses into Wood's "introduction to Southern culture" and "the joys and mishaps that so characterize [her] life as new wife and mama." Besides the drool-worthy desserts captured in minimalist excellence, the blog features photos of Wood, her husband, and their two children mid-laughter.

Both a sweet-tooth haven and a window into Wood's life, she outlines the blog's goal as follows:

"... to encourage people, to say to sa'hey make these things for yourself, not because you need cookies, but for the person you make them with and the kind of joy you spark'."

For the *person* you make them *with*. Not for the picture perfect scoop, nor the best cheese pull, or even the basic desire to eat, but for the joy of the company. Wood's purpose in food blogging, her own passion for baking, rests on a pillar of connection. Bonds more-so than blondies, are Wood's end goal.

"How your Cell Phone Hurts Your Relationships"[94]

"Feeling Lonely? Too Much Time On Social Media May Be Why"[95]

"Study Links Social Media Use to Isolation in Young Adults"[96]

The list goes on.

94 Lin, Helen Lee. 2012. "How Your Cell Phone Hurts Your Relationships". *Scientific American*. https://www.scientificamerican.com/article/how-your-cell-phone-hurts-your-relationships/.
95 Hobson, Katherine. 2017. "Feeling Lonely? Too Much Time on Social Media May Be Why". *Npr.Org*. https://www.npr.org/sections/health-shots/2017/03/06/518362255/feeling-lonely-too-much-time-on-social-media-may-be-why.
96 Willingham, AJ. 2017. "Study Links Social Media Use To Isolation In Young Adults". *CNN*. https://www.cnn.com/2017/03/06/health/social-media-isolation-study-trnd/index.html.

No, we cannot say we've entirely figured out how technology impacts our lives, but scientists and researchers have unearthed a bold, correlating line between social media use and weighty feelings of seclusion.

That's right, for all the likes and shares and thousands of friends and followers, academic spheres are releasing more and more reports attributing a heightened sense of social isolation to increased use of social media. NPR covered a report co-led by the University of Pittsburgh's Director of the Center for Research on Media, Technology, Brian Primack.[97] Primack found that, of the 1,787 U.S. adults aged 19 to 32 surveyed in the study, those who reported spending more than two hours a day on social media had "twice the odds of perceived social isolation than those who spent a half hour or less per day on those sites."

So, are Wood's efforts all for naught? Real connection cannot seriously come from our digital fountainheads of loneliness, sharing a lineage with the ringing scourge on our relationships, right? Wrong. Why? Because its food, and unique to digital food media, content need not demand its viewership turn away from the screen, it need only capture food to compel the audience to leave the screen for the grocery store or nearby deli with friends and or family in mind.

---

97 Hobson. 2017. "Feeling Lonely? Too Much Time on Social Media May Be Why". *Npr.Org.*

* * *

Once, I made a ketogenic Meyer lemon cheesecake with my mother. The ketogenic, or "keto" diet attracted popular culture's attention at the start of 2018, one of the handful of eating trends propelled into the food and nutrition world's virtual spotlight. No single article kick started this craze, but even before the ball dropped on 2018, publishers and news outlets like CNBC were predicting the ketogenic diet to be among the "foods you will be eating in 2018."[98] Its followers, like my mother, fill their plates with glorious fats like cheese, butter, avocados, some protein and scattered servings of carbs in the form of leafy greens and cauliflower, to force their bodies to the exalted "ketosis" state, a fat-blasting dream, a land of stable blood sugar and overall new heights for individual health.

For such promising diets, cheesecake rarely makes the "permitted" foods list, but the world of food-blogging and its many niches carved a place for keto and its disciples. A quick Google search brings one to a world of buttery delicacies, rising from dense almond flour dough, sweetened with a variety of zero calorie sugar replacements that save keto followers from a dessert-less world. In this corner of the Internet, my

---

98 Whitten, Sarah. 2018. "6 Foods You Will Be Eating In 2018". *CNBC*. https://www.cnbc.com/2017/12/27/6-foods-you-will-be-eating-in-2018.html.

mother found a cheesecake that compliments her dietary requirements and aids in the pursuit of her health aspirations.

Yellow-hued cake atop a firm crumbly crust carefully and specifically designed to counter its rich yet airy counterpart and completed with a thin slice of lemon cut halfway through and twisted to advertise the masterpiece's main bright attraction. Keto-dreams and prayers answered, we set to work. The recipe we found came from a blog, I Breath I'm Hungry, committed to keto and recipes that, if nothing else, dressed the keto diet up in ways that seemed to promise full bellies with a side of miracle healing and waist- trimming benefits.[99] Our search, with bag full of orange-yellow Meyer lemons sitting just to the right of our iPad screen, returned a picture of a fluffy white cheesecake undetectably different from any other "cheesecake" search Google could pull from its depths.

Our interaction followed the steps of many and home cooks and virtual foodies: search, find, drool, create. In a quest to appease extravagant cravings through extravagant restrictions, we stumbled across a world of similarly challenged eaters and cooks. The blog from which our recipe came included also a personal story, the original cook's trepidations,

---

99   Sevigny, Mellissa. 2018. "Easy Lemon Cheesecake - Low
     Carb & Keto | I Breathe I'm Hungry". *I Breathe I'm Hungry.*
     Accessed October 13. https://www.ibreatheimhungry.com/
     easy-lemon-cheesecake-low-carb-keto/.

missteps but ultimate success and deeper exploration of her website divulged hundreds more recipes to appease any other sweet tooth bound to keto diet laws. Yet, through all of our success and gratitude we never once looked at the name of the blogger, her image and blurb length biography appear as blurs on the screen's right hand side in my memory and what personal story or unique insight she revealed in the paragraphs preceding the ingredient list to which we so anxiously scrolled.

Then I listened to MIT Professor, Sherry Turkle's TED Talk, during which she appealed to the audience to preserve places, like the kitchen, for sacred screen-less time.

"I embody the central paradox," she claimed from the TED stage. As the woman who advocates for real human interaction, who asks the world to use technology to inspire our real, non-virtual lives, Sherry Turkle still loves to receive texts from her daughter.[100] We all love to use technology to feel closer to one another, to affirm our aspirational paths on the virtual plane, and declare ourselves, our relationships, our passions, our successes and even our losses from the platforms provided by statuses, updates, and stories. In Turkle's words, technology has ushered in a new philosophy:

---

100 Turkle, Sherry. 2012. *Connected, But Alone?*. Video. https://www. ted.com/talks/sherry_turkle_alone_together.

"I share therefore I am."[101] This motto leaves us seeking refuge in our carefully composed emails, texts and captions, more comfortable and capable of handling a typo than a slip of the tongue.

Turkle fears our plugged-in lives "don't only change what we do, they change who we are," and to Turkle, this future looks ominous: "I think we're setting ourselves up for trouble—trouble certainly in how we relate to each other, but also trouble in how we relate to ourselves and our capacity for self reflection... Across generations, I see that people can't get enough of each other, if and only if they can have each other at a distance, in amounts they can control."[102] But in the world Turkle outlines, where self depends on social network, the food internet glimmers optimistically.

Yes, the internet overflows with virtual communities digitally united in their love for all things vegan, or those who adore nothing more than the ease and limitless options offered by a pressure cooker, or those of us who virtually celebrate Washington DC's vibrant and varied brunch scene. Yes, there is that friend whose most recent correspondence has been to tag you, a known lover of cheese, in yet another Facebook video showcasing "A Cheese-lover's Dream."

---

101 Ibid.
102 Ibid.

Yes, these communities and this media may be where we wander when a class or meeting gets dry but one thing grounds these interactions that just might work against the socially inept world Turkle foresees. Every recipe blogged about, gooey Instagram photo, hands-in-pans video, listicle and cooking email subscription inevitably revolves around human experience. The Food Internet and its media cannot exist if no one steps away from their screens and interacts, in some way with the food, inspiring the consumer to step away from his or her own virtual self and try it-recipe, restaurant, ingredient, appliance.

Whether with friends in the trendiest restaurant or cramped in a full family kitchen, to interact with food we must remove our eyes from our screens and put our cell phones aside to hold something else in our hands. Smells, sounds, textures, and tastes engage our senses as the world evolves from the two dimensional. When these virtual communities motivate off-screen action, even if that action amounts to a recipe abandoned mid-grocery store at the prospects of a futile ingredient search or empty shelves, real world experience supersedes the virtual one and an individual still finds him or herself, though potentially tempted by the ease of the freezer section, with crumpled recipe in hand, unplugged.

My mother and I left the grocery store with three plastic bags and an ingredient list entirely crossed out. At home, we divided the recipe: I was to handle the crust while she dumped package upon package of cream cheese into the white electric mixer that has always held a place in our kitchen. We took breaks from conversation to focus on our individual efforts and we bumped into each other as we teasingly fought over and flipped through the two recipe tabs on the iPad screen. While the cheesecake was cooking, we had wine and watched TV and when the timer finally sounded, well aware our creation was far warmer than any cheesecake—keto or not— ought to be, together we fell victims to our impatience and spooned pieces onto waiting plates.

When my best friend and I ventured to Montreal in the middle of December, again we turned to the Internet. Desperate to find food and drinks worth both our money and a walk in the fierce Canadian winter wind, one search brought us to *Eater*.

You might know *Eater*, the Vox Media-owned network of food and dining websites, because you were visiting New York and needed to know your way around the city's street food, or perhaps you were craving Ramen in Montreal, or maybe you just wanted to explore the London restaurants that have opened since your last visit. The point: Eater had the news and list-icles (stories written in list form) you needed to make your way expertly around nearly any city's food and dining scene.

Tim Ebner, a freelance food writer in DC, has been contributing to *Eater* and a collection of other publications, since the early 2000s, even before Vox purchased it from Curbed Media:

"You saw a quick rise of the ubiquitous food blogger, is what I would call it—I think everyone was doing really interesting stuff but sort of in a vacuum of their own community. And *Eater*, to me, was one of the first examples where I saw them tapping into this idea of people who are supremely passionate about food but want to share it with a broader community of people, other than just their followers."

So in the early 2000s, Lockhart Steele, the founder of Curbed Media, and Ben Leventhal, the CEO of *Resy*, co-founded *Eater* as a nightlife guide for New York City. As a contributor rather than full-time employee to *Eater*, Ebner's watched *Eater* develop as a third party, relative to similar food and dining publishers, impartial to its success:

"I think they saw all of this was happening and they really wanted to capture, was the 'Well if I'm in Chicago or in L.A., I want to be immediately connected into that community and know where I should be eating, what are the cool chefs, what are the things that I should be doing as someone who is really passionate about food.' So that's, I think, how *Eater* really got its formation."

Less than ten years later, the site covers nearly twenty other cities in addition to the Big Apple. When Vox Media acquired Eater, their capacity to be an active and immediate member of any city's food community multiplied by the power of Vox's resources.

"That magic sauce of community has always carried *Eater* through," Ebner explains. When it came to be owned by Vox, *Eater* began publishing what Ebner and *Eater* call "map-stack" articles. In this story format, a list of restaurants curated by an Eater contributor, briefly described and all hyperlinked, appear next to a an interactive map. As a visitor scrolls through the list or clicks on a restaurant name, a correlating pin lights up on the adjoined map. In one page, the reader has recommendations, details, contact information and geographic location. *Eater's* maps highlight everything from "Where to Eat in And Around NYC's Koreatown" to Ebner's "12 Essential D.C. Steakhouses to Try."[103, 104]

"We realized like, to really get to know a city, you have to be able to quantify it and organize it," Ebner continues. Knowing where things are, where the best Thai food is located or

103 Kim, Sam. 2018. "Where To Eat In And Around NYC'S Koreatown". *Eater NY*. https://ny.eater.com/maps/best-koreatown-restaurants-nyc.
104 Ebner, Tim. 2018. "12 Essential D.C. Steakhouses To Try". *Eater DC*. https://dc.eater.com/maps/best-steakhouses-dc-washington-meat.

what DC neighborhoods hide New York style pizza are the knowledge bases which distinguish visitors from locals. *Eater* offers anyone a local's insight, one click away from directions to get there.

That December night, my friend and I braved only a few minutes of well-below freezing temperatures. An *Eater* map brought us quickly from apartment to vintage bar, to late night Ramen.

Turkle concludes her TED talk with one parting plea: "Now we all need to focus on the many, many ways technology can lead us back to our real lives, our own bodies, our own communities, our own politics, our own planet...Let's talk about how we can use digital technology, the technology of our dreams, to make this life the life we can love."

That technology includes the joy of creating and eating keto-genic Meyer lemon cheesecake, the blog, *Wood & Spoon*, and networks like *Eater*.

PART IV

ENGAGE

"Life itself is the proper binge."

Eating, of course, is the best part of food—smelling it, tasting it, discovering the flavors, textures, and temperatures hidden in a forkful. Knowing the heat of spice, or the rush of sweetness against the top of your tongue, listening to the ding of silverware against china or the rustle of paper bags in eager hands or the metallic crackle of aluminum foil peeled back in the midst of a busy sidewalk. The smell of browned butter, the look of cheese still melting, the resistance of a fork moving through a maze of pasta—were eating merely a task of good health, akin to brushing one's teeth, there would be none of this and no joy found in it.

Undoubtedly, meals are daily rituals of nourishment keeping hearts pumping, brains clear, and stomachs silent. But with herbs, spices, and ingredients we've invoked precise senses and added a dose of sentiment to the things we make and eat. We've made food a celebration, a tradition, and an art for when we eat, we must make. Whether it be a decision or a recipe, something must come into existence to arrive on our plates.

Our screens can capture much—color, the look of steam, the sound of searing, diners' verbal and visual reactions. They can share it all across the world, they can promote or destroy a restaurant, and give new life to age-old recipes but they cannot duplicate the smell of lamb chops fresh out of the oven nor the docile satisfaction of a full belly. The best of food media acknowledges this unsurpassable barrier. It submits to authentic experience and brings people to the table.

CHAPTER 9

THE OLD IS NEW AGAIN

—

Has the world ever been without some form of food media?

When man was quite terminally lost for words in the pre-historic era, rough drawings captured the scene of the hunt. Ancient Egyptian pictographs feature workers pulling wheat from a field, Iranian relics from the ruins of Persepolis bare the images of slaves carrying food and wine, 2nd century floor mosaics emulating the celebratory chaos of a feast's aftermath speckle Europe.[105, 106] Was The Last Supper not a feast after all? Madame de Sévigné's of King Louis's France describes, in her letters, 'pyramids of fruit' so huge doorways

105 Butler, Sharon. 2017. "A Brief History Of Food As Art". *Smith-sonian Magazine*. https://www.smithsonianmag.com/travel/food-art-cultural-travel-180961648/.

106 *Relief: Two Servants Bearing Food And Drink*. n.d. Limestone. New York, New York: The Metropolitan Museum of Art.

were 'raised' to accommodate them.[107] Meléndez painted pale green melons and bright yellow citrus with a thick pink cut of salmon and Cezanne painted peaches.[108, 109, 110] By the time Julia Child's face and hands (for she gets the real credit for pioneering the over-the-shoulder cooking shot) graced 20th century screens and shelves, the world was warming up for the sprint of internet connection.

In the popularity of Child's show and the successful debut of still-popular food publishers like *Bon Appetite* and *Good Housekeeping*, perhaps we see the first glimpse of our food-pornographic selves. But these are late manifestations of food media, at best the early signs of obsessions, not the marker of a new interest. I do not feign historic credentials grander than long-standing interest and successfully completed undergraduate courses (though a final paper expounding upon the history of wine in King Louis XVI's France helped achieve this end). Yet, the evidence in defense of a human impulse to capture what we spread across our tables and put in our mouths stacks high—a teetering compilation

107 Sévigné, Marie de Rabutin-Chantal, and Leonard Tancock. 1982. *Selected Letters Of Madame De Sevigne ; Translated With An Introduction By Leonard Tancock*. Harmondsworth: Penguin.

108 Meléndez, Luiz. 1772. *The Afternoon Meal (La Merienda)*. Oil on canvas. New York, New York: The Metropolitan Museum of Art.

109 Meléndez, Luiz. 1772. *Still Life With Salmon, Lemon And Three Vessels*. Oil on canvas. Madrid, Spain: Museo Del Prado.

110 Cézanne, Paul. 1905. *Still Life With Apples And Peaches*. Oil on canvas. Washington, D.C.: The National Gallery.

of art and articles, magazines, newspaper sections, television shows, and now hashtags.

Perhaps the birth of widespread "foodie" culture has been wrongly credited to millennials. It was not they who popularized the sharing of food content, it was simply they who first did so on Instagram.

What's behind it all? Documentation certainly, a facet the online "foodie" world has only heightened. But a continued stream of cookbook releases and billions of recipes available suggest practicality, the education in the preparation and procedure of a dish, propels food media. After all, what would food be if we did not make, play with, and eat it.

* * *

A grandmother kneads dough at the kitchen counter. Sunlight streams in as clouds of flour burst into the air and catch the light that spills past the bowl of tomatoes freshly picked from the garden. Here, at her elbow, is where many learned what food should be, leaning over grandmother's shoulder to watch exactly how to push your palms into the sticky risen dough while listening for the sauce on the stove to bubble at the right pitch. Here, many learned not how to cook well.

But not all enjoyed the luxury of a culinary adept grand-mother and not all grandmothers ever cared to cater dishes far beyond their specialties. So, while some home cooks first mastered a well-roasted chicken at grandmother's elbow, many crack open a new cookbook, and persuaded by a gloss-finished page, to begin what can best be described as an attempt.

For this home cook, a cookbook's instructions can be little more than vague suggestions prompting a row of freshly opened search tabs. In a quest to discover what exactly seared, spatchcocked, or smoked chicken are, how each should look, and how they are different from each other, a cookbook can disappoint and feeds an envy of the cook trained by gener-ational wisdom and live experience. This is the category of cook to which David Ellner once belonged.

Over a decade ago, the former president of Digital and Busi-ness Development for 19 Entertainment, home to *American Idol*, was gifted Thomas Keller's cookbook, *Bouchon*. The book opens with Keller's suggestion that everyone know how to make a roast chicken. This was a feat Ellner himself had never previously attempted, but as he told *Food52*, "I jumped in, made my first roast chicken, and was hooked," David joined the ranks of cookbook cooks.[111]

---

111 Wilbur, Kenzi. 2013. "David Ellner, Founder Of The Panna Cooking App (And A Giveaway!)". *Food52*. https://food52.com/

As he made more and more recipes, more and more questions arose. Is chopped carrot the same as a diced carrot? Will substituting liquid measuring cups for dry measuring cups ruin everything? Why was the meal David slaved over for the third time not identical to the photo on the cookbook's glossy page? Out of these frustrations, came *Panna*.

Panna, originally offered as a "video food magazine," is now a website, app and "video cookbook." It offers its subscribers over 300 hours (and growing) of video recipes guided by award winning chefs. From Andrew Zimmerman to Michael Solomonov, the viewer learns by watching the masters and literally seeing the dish develop before them. Ellner wanted to make something authentic, authoritative, and reliable, the answer to all of his own home-cooking qualms. Through *Panna*, he turned to the methods we've used to for centuries— learning from the best. *Panna* gathers some of the world's best chefs, and puts them before a camera to give their recipes stripped of all the "chefy" stuff and preserving the recipe's core, made un-intimidating to any home chef following along.

In one of Ellner's favorite videos, James Beard award-winning chef, restaurateur, and author, Nancy Silverton guides the viewer through the intimidating process of making a tart,

blog/5423-david-ellner-founder-of-the-panna-cooking-app-and-a-giveaway.

specifically a brown butter tart with berries. Below the video is a list of ingredients accompanied by the instructions, just as you would see in a cookbook, but with *Panna*, there's a high quality video and Silverton herself besides it all.

Silverton's video, like all of *Panna's* videos, is sectioned off according to the recipe's steps so the viewer can watch the whole recipe at once, or skip to and pause on certain steps. As Silverton dusts her work surface, her years of experience show in the quick, confident and effective flick of her forearm. In three motions, she covers the white marble counter in flour. While Silverton speaks to the camera about the importance of keeping the dough cool by barely using your palms in kneading, her wrists and hands move in subtle coordinated movements that send the dough leaping in quick bursts between countertop and fingertips. While the butter is browning, the video hones in on the sound of butter bubbling on the stove and when Silverton says "pound the dough" before slamming the chilled dough repeatedly with her rolling pin, little is left to the imagination - you see she really means "pound' it. Following along with Nancy herself, the viewer's own brown butter tart has a high chance of coming out just as well.

As Ellner describes the platform, "It's a tool to make something delicious for someone you love," in the same way that grandma leans over the old wooden table to make the same dish she's been making for years. The luxury of learning at the elbow of the best comes to life through *Panna*, and the Vivian Howard-hosted video recipe for black bean glazed salmon with ginger cabbage received the James Beard Foundation award for Best Instructional Video.[112, 113] The chefs Ellner puts in front of the camera are the ultimate authorities, in Ellner's words, "they've made so many mistakes, they know when it's just right and when it's not. It's hard to describe." But even *Panna's* videos can't capture the entire magic of a master chef at work.

"We can get so much right," Ellner explains, "when a chef says whip something to soft peaks, 'soft peaks' is not a descriptive term." The camera can capture it, but it can't necessarily capture every movement and variable that makes the soft peaks the exact ones that an outstanding chef, like Nancy Zimmerman would make.

Even Ellner, who has made most of the recipes featured on *Panna*, can't get the tortillas Gabriela the chef-owner of nine restaurants in Mexico and San Francisco's Cala, to be exactly like those Cámara makes in *Panna's* Mexican Street Food

112 Panna Cooking. 2018. *Black Bean-Glazed Salmon With Cabbage By Vivian Howard*. Video. Accessed October 14. https://www.pannacooking.com/recipes/black-bean-glazed-salmon-ginger-cabbage-vivian-howard/.

113 Jackson, Drew. 2018. "James Beard Award Given To Vivian Howard-Hosted Video. Next Up, The Daytime Emmys.". *Newsobserver*. https://www.newsobserver.com/living/article210047779.html.

class. He makes them by watching exactly what Cámara did so he knows what standard his ought to live up to. His are good, not Cámara-good, but they're good and the point remains—he still made them. With *Panna*, Ellner solved what he saw as the problem of the traditional cookbook, using the digital to give greater life to food.

The birth of *Panna* does not invite the death of cookbooks, but it ushers in a new kind of cookbook, one divorced from paper pages. The printed cookbook has not lost its merit, remaining one of the few printed genres unwavering in the dawn of the digital era, but Ellner is not alone in re-imagining the cookbook.

In 1961, the man credited as the "father of modern restaurant criticism," published a cookbook.[114] The cookbook came from a then-regional paper but claimed a spot on the list of national best-sellers for over a decade. Nearly sixty years later, over three million of its copies and editions scatter the world and sales haven't stopped yet.[115] The book is, after all, Craig Claiborne's *The New York Times Cookbook*.

---

114 Martin, Adam. 2012. "Meet The Father Of Modern Restaurant Criticism". *The Atlantic*. https://www.theatlantic.com/entertainment/archive/2012/05/meet-father-modern-restaurant-criticism/328406/.

115 "The New York Times Cook Book". 2018. *Amazon. Com*. Accessed October 14. https://www.amazon.com/New-York-Times-Cook-Book/dp/0060160101.

When Sam Sifton was named the successor to Clairborne's position as the *NYT's* Food Editor, *The New York Times* had already accumulated an archive of recipes dating, digitally, back to the 1980s. The archive was a "dead letter office," Sifton claimed, filled with article assets stripped of pictures, convenience and joy. But in their gloom and barrenness, Sifton, alongside many of his colleagues, saw opportunity to emulate Claiborne's analog *NYT Cookbook* feat on the digital plane. If the thousands of "dead" recipes could be organized into a database, and rejuvenated with photos and stories, they could live a new life of new functionality. The mission was a bet, it would require much tedious work, even outside help. Yet, in Sifton's mind it was an easy bet to make. Claiborne changed the way people understood the New York Times, the paper was no longer a regional or metropolitan publication, there was no need to let an international archive wilt rather than continue the legacy of the *New York Times's Cookbook*. The process promised *NYT Food* and the *NYT* itself a new facet: *New York Times* Cooking.

The idea was good but the work was not. The recipes existing by the thousands, if not millions, needed to be rendered as data and individually vitalized with a bright photo and top note. As "assets" the recipes were divorced from their original stories. As he explained, if Sam Sifton had traveled to the Delmarva peninsula to learn how to make Anabelle Nuelle's famous fried chicken, he would publish an article about the experience and our conversation and the recipe would conclude the article as a post-script, the "how-to" of the experience. The archived recipe assets amounted solely to that post-script, lobbed off from the story that explained their origin and lent them their authority. To transfer these lifeless amputations online and restored, was a long and tedious task, costing *The New York Times* months of labor, but at its end, *New York Times Cooking* was founded.

Now, *The New York Times Cooking* welcomes millions of visitors each month and is home to thousands of recipes (with more added each week). Just as *Claiborne's Cookbook* brought a new world of cooking to homes across America and made national a regional newspaper, Sifton's *NYT Cooking* brings its users to a new relationship with food and the joys of cooking on digitized scale.

"In a way, there are lots of people looking to see how a digital future is a refutation of where we are now," as if we are "entering into a brave new world" in the digital sphere, Sifton explained. "*NYT Cooking* is a kind of conservative act, that recalls the *NYT Cookbook*… the same challenges that I face, Claiborne faced… We want to teach people to think of us as a really good source, not just for news about the world, what's going on in theater, but for what to cook and how to prepare it."

The bold red banner search bar of *New York Times Food* promising access to thousands of recipes all vibrant, and photographed in such a way that 'feasible' and 'outstanding' melt into 'try this yourself,' and inevitably spark assumptions of 'new'. We take these assumptions as compelling evidence to declare printed cookbooks a thing of the past, on its way out and never to return again. But, as Sifton underscores, could not be further from the truth. *New York Times Cooking* stands on the shoulders of the greatest cookbooks. It was inspired by them and it aims to do precisely what the cookbooks of old do with new tools for larger audiences. The end goal remains: Inspire people to try a new meal, to push their comfort zones and create. The results do not have to be perfect, but Sifton and his team do not demand perfection, they simply suggest you "come and hang out," in Sifton's words, make some good food, spend time with others and enjoy yourself.

In Ellner and Sifton's work, the cookbook tradition lives on. The legacy of food, the stories behind a dish, the techniques necessary to make it just right are all preserved but the platform it exists on has expanded to include two more: video and online database.

·

CHAPTER 10

THE TRUST TEST

—

"Bon appétit!"—the epicurean's boxing bell. At its ding, napkins fall into laps and hands grab forks in excited anticipation. Literally, the French phrase means something along the lines of "good appetite" but dining rendered the phrase a sentiment, and the English speaking world hijacked it to fill the colloquial void for which "enjoy your meal" simply won't suffice.

In addition to this practical application, the phrase became the namesake of sixty-two year old food and entertainment publisher, *Bon Appétit*. Today, its published version appears on the doorsteps of thousands of homes across the country, and its digital audience numbers in the two millions, promising each a glimpse of "life through the lens of food." The website features everything from recipes, culinary stories and articles, restaurant guides, a podcast, and, like all good digital food publishers, videos. Online, the publisher has extended itself in pieces, each geared to connect with one audience over another. Healthy-ish is for the health concerned who won't sacrifice it all, Basically is for stove or oven intimidated,

As digital director, Polis acts as guiding hand for the digital content *Bon Appetit* offers its readership, helping to lead the brand through the ever shifting digital terrain and keep cohesive the *Bon Appetit* voice running throughout. No degree or special training program exist to teach one exactly how to do this, but Polis can claim the next best thing—firsthand experience in all the shifts and growth spurts the Food Internet. For where Polis's career began is where many describe the genesis of the Food Internet, the prime of the personal blog.

If you ask Polis when she started working in digital food media, she'll tell you she started "before it was cool," in 2007 with *TheNibble*, a startup website that reviewed gourmet food products. Then, her work was niche, the kind of job family and friends ask for an explanation about or raise their eyebrows and emit an "oh, interesting" before moving the conversation along. As editorial assistant, Polis curated product reviews and glossaries, and managed all online newsletters, so by "happy accident" as Polis describes, her first exposure to food media was digital. At the time, anyone seeking to make a name for him or herself in the home cook world was

told to "start a blog!" with the optimistic pep of a not-yet
saturated space. "Blogs and websites weren't like they are
today," Polis explains, but by 2010, after Polis returned from
grad school in Italy, something had changed.

Polis's parents always supported her but before her time
abroad their support came from a place that was arguably
generated more from a place of unconditional, involuntary
parental love. What was a hesitant support, a nod and agree-
ment that her job was "cool(ish)" changed three years after
Polis's first job. "Every single friend and their kids wanted to
get in on it," Polis describes, their daughter's job held a sort of
social currency. The qualifying "ish" fell permanently away,
Polis's career transitioned officially to "cool."

From here, Polis moved on to work for The James Beard
Foundation, then as The Huffington Post's Food Editor,
before landing in *Bon Appetite*'s digital team in 2014.

"When I started, there were more print editors than digital,"
Polis explains, "now there are more digital."

The transition in *Bon Appétit's* staffing captures a far greater
adjustment than HR. For over half a century, the publisher
created a printed legacy of food media and in less than a
decade, its audience demanded digital. As she describes it,
Polis now worked for a publisher with "phenomenally good

print product in an environment where people aren't looking for print," nor was *Bon Appétit* alone in these growing pains. Rather, any publisher founded before the dawn of the popular internet sought to overcome the same challenges: transition smoothly between print and digital, leverage new technologies and platforms while maintaining a its voice, keep readership up but appeal to an ever growing audience, and oh by the way, there's no choice but to fight for audiences' ever diminishing attention.[116]

As a digital editor, these challenges serve as Polis's daily to-do list. In facing them, she draws from a digitally native career, one molded by the Food Internet's own growth pattern. Yet, her golden rule gathered from years of experience boils down not to a preferred posting time or video length, but a single, human truth—"trust, everything is contingent on trust."

* * *

In 2011, Professor Patrick O. Brown of Stanford University's Biochemistry department, world-renowned geneticist and Howard Hughes Medical Institute Investigator swore to battle the enormous environmental devastation wreaked by the

---

116 McSpadden, Kevin. 2015. "You Now Have a Shorter Attention Span Than a Goldfish". *Time*. http://time.com/3858309/attention-spans-goldfish/.

production of animal food products.[117, 118] Cognizant that the lure of a juicy burger fresh from the grill or the satisfying spoonful of a granola-topped yogurt pose significant counterarguments to those supporting a plant-based diet, Brown determined to find a solution which left all, from meat lovers to the environmentalists, happy. His villain loomed large: centuries of palattes and dinner tables groomed to crave a plate filled with bite after bite of meat, millions of burger loving loyal consumers, but Brown brought with him to the fight an idea, a reputable scientific background, and compromise almost too good to be true. In 2011, Brown brought to the battle, Impossible Foods Inc.

In an open letter posted on Impossible Food's website, Brown lays out his mission to: "enable the world to continue to enjoy the foods they love and increasingly demand, without catastrophic damage to the environment."[119] Too good to be true?

Brown continues by saying Impossible Food will, "invent a better way to transform plants into delicious, nutritious, safe and affordable meat, fish and dairy foods that consumers

---

117 "Pat Brown". 2018. *TEDMED*. https://www.tedmed.com/speakers/show?id=526389.

118 "Mission | Impossible Foods". 2018. *Impossible Foods*. Accessed October 14. https://impossiblefoods.com/mission.

119 Pat Brown, Impossible Foods. 2018. "Open Letter From The CEO". Accessed October 15. https://www.impossiblefoods.com/letter-from-the-ceo/.

love. Then let the consumer choose. If we do our job right, the market will take care of the rest."[120] A world with bellies full and happy from a meat meal that was, in truth, not meat. A not-meat-meat that promised to appeal to all consumer senses, ethics and palettes included, and so tasty the animal foods dominating the markets fade to history. This was the impossible compromise Brown sought, an idea that became the Impossible Burger. The magic behind it? Heme.

Heme, as described by Brown, is an "iron containing molecule that's essential for life on Earth... [it is] in every plant and animal, humans have been eating heme every day since the first human walked on Earth" and best of all, "the reason that animal tissues (meat) tastes like meat and unlike any vegetable, is that animal tissue contain hundreds to thousands-fold more heme than plant tissues" heme is what makes meat taste meat-y.[121]

The Impossible Burger, Impossible Food's flagship item, combines heme, genetically engineered from yeast to be identical to the heme humans have always consumed in meat, with simple, natural ingredients including wheat protein, coconut oil, and potato protein. The product complies fully with U.S. Food and Drug Administration regulations, according to their website, "compared to cows, the Impossible Burger

120 Ibid.
121 Ibid.

uses 95% less land, 74% less water, and creates 87% less greenhouse gas emissions."[122] Impossible Foods accomplished the impossible—a plant based meat that mimics the beef-eating experience carnivorous consumers know and love, down to the mouth watering sizzle of burger on grill.

But the final step of Brown's quest, to beat out the animal product market with plant-based alternatives, requires burger lovers to venture away from the standard burger, and cheat on the loyal relationship of man to meat for an entirely new kind of meat. Impossible Burger's greatest battle would be a marketing battle. As Lexi Cotcamp, Brand Marketing Manager at Impossible Foods, describes, people have preconceived notions of "what food is and isn't" and Impossible Burger aims to re-define what the world considers 'meat.' This overhaul demands a comprehensive marketing strategy, heavy in digital media like Instagram gifs and Facebook videos which show off the look and sizzle of an Impossible Burger flipped on a hot grill, mouth-watering photos, and emails. Ultimately, Lexi and her co-workers favor one platform over all others: real life.

Digital campaigns highlight all but the Impossible Burger's most convincing feature: taste. Sure the Impossible Burger looks and sounds like a burger, but it can only obtain true

---

122 "Mission | Impossible Foods". 2018. *Impossible Foods*. Accessed October 14. https://impossiblefoods.com/mission.

acceptance amongst beef-burger lovers if it tastes, smells and copies the texture of animal-based meat. So the Impossible Burger Marketing team totes one motto: tasting is believing.

Impossible Foods hosts demonstrations to sway the most dogged of critics. At a demonstration, an Impossible Food representative combines each plant based ingredient in a bowl, offering guests a bite of each ingredient before it is tossed into the large bowl. Then, magically, right before visitors' eyes, those plants transform to meat. No puff of smoke or magic wand, but by simply mixing the ingredients, the plant based ingredients daring guests taste-tested, become grown meat ready for the griddle. There is, of course, a grill at the ready. The meat is tossed onto the grill's hot surface and guests endure the symphony of crackling sizzle as the meat cooks, then, taste buds too are persuaded. With every happy mouthful, Impossible Foods and its burger are vetted, and Brown's dragon falls one step closer to annihilation. Mouthfuls become rave reviews as, person by person, the plant-based burger enters cultural dictionaries and dialogues under "meat."

* * *

In 2016, *Bon Appetit* covered the Impossible Burger in the article, "A Fake-Meat Burger So Realistic It Fooled My Entire Family" but this is not the only point of intersection between the two.[123] Food on the digital plane is food compromised, confined to just two of its dimensions. Impossible Foods Inc., like most food industry actors, knows the importance of having a digital presence, but the story of the Impossible Burger, now available around the country, could not claim such an optimistic luster on the digital plane alone. To find its place in the food scene, it had to earn diners' trust as a viable alternative to meat. *Bon Appetit* too earns its reputation by relying ultimately on the trust of consumers.

Polis defines *Bon Appetit* as a "reliable authority," with a voice more consistent with a peer than a teacher. But the publisher garners a loyal audience by emphasizing the "reliable" facet of its content: "as soon as someone goes to your site and tries a recipe that doesn't work or reads an article that oversells, they won't come back."

The reputation of *Bon Appetite*, like Impossible Burger, lies in the offline experience of the consumer. Neither could proceed if that experience undermined the reputation, for both have converted their consumers from believers to knowers— certain in the quality of their content or product.

---

123 Chaey, Christina. 2016. "The Fake-Meat Burger So Realistic It Fooled My Entire Family". *Bon Appetit*. https://www.bonappetit.com/entertaining-style/trends-news/article/impossible-burger-fake-meat.

Trust. Whether grilling meat on the barbecue as your father and his father before have, or seating yourself in a restaurant on the whim of a restaurant review, or choosing to order a 'meatless' burger, trust is at the center of what we choose to eat and make. Flooded by thousands, if not millions of digital food resources, what better filter than offline dependability? In the wake of the digital revolution, trust did not lose its premium, it solidified it.

CHAPTER 11

THE ENGAGEMENT EMPIRE

———

"Food porn," "hands in pans," "stunt food," or whatever else one might call it—there's something about the slow, gooey cheese pulls and perfectly sliced pieces of cake lifted to slowly reveal layers of cake encased in butter cream frosting. Mid newsfeed scroll, these videos offer a two minute or less escape into cooking, a DIY world saturated in color and dominated by anonymous hands with white bold print to guide the viewer through.

Frequently, we encounter these videos via Buzzfeed's *Tasty*. Self-described, *Tasty* is the "world's largest food network" where each visitor can "search, watch, and cook every single *Tasty* recipe and video ever." Launched in 2015, the media company's Facebook page counts 96 million (and growing) followers, not including the specialized offshoots of the platform including "Tasty Vegetarian," "Proper Tasty" (the British compliment), "Tasty Japan," "Tasty Miam" (the French offshoot), and more.

Though other media companies use their own renditions of the hands-in-pans short form video, *Tasty* receives popular credit. Even when the appeal of Facebook food videos seemed wavered, as reported by *Digiday* journalist Max Willens late in 2017, *Tasty's* enormous reach and reputation kept the platform premium. As Willens reported, a partnership with *Tasty* cost "twice as much —300,000—as a program that included three videos, three pieces of written sponsored content and a catch of supporting media offered by a competitor, Tasting Table."[124] With over 207 million views on *Tasty's* "Sliders Four Ways" Facebook video alone, the price might just be worth it.[125]

Whether showcasing an easy to clean One-Pot Chicken Alfredo or an eye catching Rainbow Crepe Cake many of *Tasty's* videos come in a standard form: a three-second flash forward to the recipe's last step and the ever pleasing slow

---

124 Willens, Max. 2017. "Signs That Facebook Food Videos Are Losing Their Luster - Digiday". *Digiday*. https://digiday.com/media/signs-facebook-food-videos-losing-luster/.

125 Tasty. 2018. *Sliders 4 Ways*. Video. Accessed October 14. https://www.tasty.co/compilation/sliders-4-ways#4ldradw.

pull or fork lift of the final product before the video jumps into the recipe's first step. White instructions noting each ingredient appear as the camera's overhead shot films a pair of hands executing each step. The videos focus on the food, not the maker and originally, his or her face never appeared. The videos don't need sound to be enjoyed because Facebook's autoplay feature includes no sound, but if a viewer unmutes the video, he or she hears instrumental music, played unobtrusively on repeat.

According to a former employee, a single person produces a video in whole, shooting, cooking and editing videos on his or her own frequently, on his or her own. *Tasty* employees are young, making digital natives responsible for digital content creation. Like industrial mechanics, *Tasty's* model is formulaic, fast and efficient. Mass produced, the "food porn," as its frequently dubbed, circulates to millions.

Cari Romm, in her 2015 Atlantic article titled "What 'Food Porn' Does to the Brain" describes food porn:

"Food porn is defined in part by the senses that it is a visual experience of something that other people can smell and taste. Food porn, as Amanda Simpson, the creator of the site Food Porn Daily, told *The Daily Meal* in 2010, is "anything that makes me drool"—something that, at its best, should manufacture a desire that it can't satisfy."[126]

Unsatisfiable but appealing, the scientists Romm surveys claim the mouth watering videos *Tasty* manufactures can do anything from elicit appetites to substitute for the real thing. Either way, the videos stop thumbs mid-scroll and collect millions upon millions of views.

Some criticize BuzzFeed for this. In my own conversations, I have heard accusers label the videos as gimmicky, commercial, and cold. Addictive in the same way a family size bag of chips while binge watching TV shows might be addictive. Easy to consume, quick, delicious but not a fine meal you would savor. Still, *Tasty's* Facebook following equivalent to nearly 30% of the United States' population, was cultivated with no personalities, no subscriber communities, no well-know newsletters.

In an interview at Stream USA 2016, a conference bringing together hundreds of creative, media, and technology leaders to discuss the future of technology and creativity, Ashley McCollum, the General Manager of BuzzFeed's *Tasty*, spoke about the strategy behind *Tasty's* initial success:

---

126 Romm, Cari. 2015. "What 'Food Porn' Does To The Brain". *The Atlantic*. https://www.theatlantic.com/health/archive/2015/04/what-food-porn-does-to-the-brain/390849/.

First, she pointed out that *Tasty*, as the food vertical extension of BuzzFeed, centers on "social... When you look at a video and scroll through the comments and you see people tagging their husband and saying 'Let's do this, this weekend,' 'tagging their whole families, all with the same last name, and saying 'Let's make this Sunday night'," that's the goal. Accordingly, the secret to success is making shareable content, content that, as in McCollum's examples is inherently social. "... make [content] with the hope in mind that people will use it to connect with other people, that we believe is the best growth strategy."[127]

McCollum and BuzzFeed are not the only people to understand this. Jason Peterson, the CCO and chairman of creative ad agency, Havas, and photographer with over a million Instagram followers who was asked to photograph Obama's farewell speech, does too. Peterson places special emphasis on the social facet of social media, "It's like a party," Peterson explains, " Don't just stand there and say, why isn't anyone talking to me? Why does no one care about me? Go out there and be social." Create content worthy of being shared.

But if this is the goal, social sharing, what role can the faceless overhead shot play? "Amputated hands" as some have

---

127 McCollum, Ashley. 2016. 5 MIN TALK: Making Sharable Content with Ashley McCollum, General Manager, Tasty, Buzzfeed Jonathan Cloonan Interview by . In person. Stream USA 2016.

deemed the digits starring in *Tasty's* recipe format, lack a person and thus can offer no sense of connection. Replacing a voice guiding the viewer through the recipe with momentary abbreviated instructions leaves no room for any story about the culture from which a dish comes or the inspiration behind a recipe to be told. The videos seem, in a phrase, superficial. But McCollum and the team at *Tasty* see the hands behind *Tasty* very differently.

"If you look at the space, 99% of food media is made by professionals. You have Martha Stewart in a kitchen you can't afford making a crème brûlée you may not ever be able to make, but 99% of food is made by amateurs. So what is that difference between the two? Why does food media not represent the reality of the food experience most people have. So we think that that big space is really what we [BuzzFeed Tasty] are going after."[128] This is where the *Tasty's* famous anonymous hands come into play.

McCollum continues:

"If you watch a traditional food show, a cooking show is shot from this angle," McCollum gestures horizontally to recall the hundreds of open facing kitchens of Food Network filmed as if the camera were a guest observing the host

---

128 Hustle Co. 2018. *Ashley Mccollum | GM Of Tasty @ Buzzfeed.* Video. https://www.youtube.com/watch?v=y7RcwQ4ni1o.

cook.[129] "You can kind of watch it passively on the couch," McCollum continues, "Our media is really made from the angle of the audience, from the chef. So, you're really looking down over your phone just like the angle of the video, so it's *your* hands, it's *your* hands cooking it, so it's a totally different point of view."[130]

Where traditional food media aims to be observed, arguably a form of entertainment, *Tasty's* videos are shot to be practical and instructional—precisely the sort of guidance the 99% of amateur food preparers might need.

Where competitors and critics see disconnect, McCollum and the *Tasty* team see approachability. The overhead shot characteristic of *Tasty*, according to McCollum and her team, is not a mark of anonymous detachment but of inspiring potential in the audience, inviting them to perceive the video's hands as their own. Making an argument for connection and real world action by appealing to brevity, convenience, but most importantly, the audience's experience and desire to act.

* * *

---

129 Ibid.
130 Ibid.

For the majority of my writing process, *Tasty* was the final piece of the jigsaw puzzle that refused to fit no matter which way I turned it or how forcefully I tried to get it to fit. It emerged as the counterexample to the wholesome roots for which I have argued throughout the duration of this book. Where most digital food media are community oriented, or heightened by individual personality, or bettered by a sense of personal connection, *Tasty* is anonymous, speedy and mass-produced. Where most have stories, *Tasty* has cyclic music not dissimilar to modern elevator music though the videos need not be played with any sound at all. So what's the difference? Is there something we have missed? Have I been wrong the entire time? Perhaps, as Sam Sifton once suggested to me, there is a psychological reaction to this form of food video, that maybe there is more than we anticipated in the "foodporn" title *Tasty* so often wins. But then again, the Food Internet overflows with content nearly identical to BuzzFeed's style of videos, so there must be something there—right? Kind of.

My frustrations reached a near frightening peak as I wrapped up the research portion of my writing. I could not unearth the secret to *Tasty's* success in any of my interviews or personal research. In a word, I was stumped. I was very stumped, the kind of stumped you get when you've tried nearly everything and a single media outlet threatens to push your entire book and theory off the tracks. Then, I found one last video.

Two hands pour two cups of water into a pan on a stove top, "I'm going to make fried chicken" a voice declares holding the sharp vowels of "fried" for a little longer, in a way that could only twist the speaker's mouth into a smile. 1 cup of Kosher salt goes into the pan next "Fried chicken for me is such an iconic recipe that speaks to American culture, very often Southern American culture," the voice says as the same hands pour the salted water into a much larger pan followed by 6 cups of ice water. The hands start placing eight uncooked chicken thighs and drumsticks into the water "I want to listen to some really good music" the voice says this time holding into the "r" of 'really,' "sit outside, eat it with my hands and just share it with some friends, you know. That's living, that's good life." The voice stops for a moment as the pot of chicken and water is transferred to the refrigerator for ninety minutes, smooth music takes over to allow the associations the voice just described to unfold as one scene in the audience's mind's eye. Sitting outside with really good music, fried chicken eaten by hand and shared amongst friends, perhaps in the warmth and leisure of a classic American summer."[131] The good life, indeed.

These are the hands, voice, and perspective of Marcus Samuelsson. A famous chef and restaurateur, Samuelsson has starred on some of the Food Network's most popular

---

131 Tasty. 2016. *Fried Chicken As Made By Marcus Samuelsson*. Video. https://www.youtube.com/watch?v=k7MafUNvuXs.

television shows including *Iron Chef, Chopped All-Stars*, Top Chef *Masters, 24 Hour Restaurant Battle, The Martha Stewart Show, The Today Show* and even his own show, *The Inner Chef,* airing on Discovery Network.[132] Not only is Samuelsson a three time James Beard Award winning chef, but he served the Obama administration's first state dinner for the first family, Prime Minister of India Manmohan Singh, and four hundred other guests as a guest chef at the White House. Most impressive of all, Samuelsson is the head chef and co-creator of the acclaimed Red Rooster Harlem.[133] In an interview with Recode, a technology website focusing on Silicon Valley, he dives deeper into the background surrounding Red Rooster's conception.[134]

When Samuelsson and his co-creator, Andrew Chapman, opened Red Rooster Harlem in 2011, his intentions were bigger than a brick and mortar restaurant. "There are a couple of things that I always was intrigued by," he says, and his curiosity began with a single question: "How can I change the foot traffic of dining and the foot traffic of the conversation?" "I felt it was just very flat," he continues "And this

---

132 "Marcus Samuelsson Bio". 2018. *Foodnetwork.Com*. https://www. foodnetwork.com/profiles/talent/marcus-samuelsson/bio.

133 Ibid.

134 Code Media. 2017. *Full Video: Tasty GM Ashley Mccollum And Chef Marcus Samuelsson At Code Media*. Video. https://www. recode.net/2017/3/18/14958934/video-watch-food-buzzfeed-tasty-gm-ashley-mccollum-chef-marcus-samuelsson-code-media.

was something that I thought about when I was working in France, and being in Japan and traveling around the world. I'm like—why is it only that French Food is accepted fine dining?"[135]

Since the early 2000s, that has changed and slowly, other foods—from Mediterranean falafels to Korean barbeque—have made their way into fine dining. As Samuelsson observed this slow change, his questions evolved to confront a second space he perceived in the culinary world. "...Then it was something like, when you want to show your dish or show your daily special, why do you have to wait for like the local paper or *New York Times* on Wednesday to write about it? Right? There has to be a different way." When Samuelsson opened Red Rooster Harlem, these two—a platform for new falvors and an in-house platform to share food news—were in the forefront of his mind. "When I had the opportunity to open Red Rooster in Harlem, I started two things. I was like, 'I'm not going to open a restaurant without not starting a media space. So I actually started Food Republic in the basement of Red Rooster at the same time."[136] Food Republic is the digital side of Samuelsson's vision.

Food Republic quickly became a staple of the digital lifestyle scene in the United States and across the globe, featuring

135 Ibid.
136 Ibid.

interviews with prominent chefs and personalities, stories about the culture and lifestyles surrounding food and drink, and recipes from chefs, cookbook authors, and the Food Republic Test kitchen. Across the website's screen reads the following quote from Samuelsson himself: "We're all on a journey and it's about evolution and we're in evolution with our guess. My purpose as an immigrant, as a chef of color, I always thought about how I can do something that helps that."[137] The simultaneous establishment of Food Republic and Red Rooster were the answers to his own questions: food and media. As both unfolded, the affinity of food and media grew more apparent. "It was tech guys in that room, and the cooks in that room," gesturing with his hands to separate but neighboring spaces in the air, "I realized it was pretty similar—highly passionate people, very expensive to build both," he jokes, "but I will always want to share my one point of view," and "if you're going to open up a restaurant today, if you're going to have a food dialogue with the public today, it's not either or, it's both," its traditional restaurant and new media platforms, united.[138]

In the previously mentioned fried chicken recipe Samuelsson walks the viewer through isn't his typical cooking show—it's a two minute long BuzzFeed *Tasty* video.

---

137 Ibid.
138 Ibid.

"So, I'm from Ethiopia" Samuelsson's voice continues as his hands place a glass baking dish beneath the camera and into which he pours two cups of buttermilk, three- quarter cups of coconut milk and sprinkles two garlic cloves.[139] "The main spice dish in Ethiopia is called 'berbere' so for my chicken shake the main ingredient is berbere. It's a beautiful sort of mild chili blend," into a separate bowl goes berbere, hot smoked paprika, ground cumin, white pepper, celery powder and garlic. "This is to make sure that the chicken gets the smoky, beautiful, spicy flavor that makes our fried chicken so very special." For a moment, the top of Samuelsson's Red Rooster Harlem hat blocks the camera as Samuelsson leans in to sniff his Ethiopian spice blend.[140]

At Red Rooster "Fried Yard Bird," much like the recipe Samuelsson walks through, is one of the menu's main attractions. In their own words, Red Rooster "serves comfort food celebrating the roots of American cuisine and the diverse culinary traditions of the neighborhood."[141] The addition of Ethiopian berbere makes Red Rooster's fried chicken unique, a standout amongst the numerous other fried chicken options, including Sylvia's—what Samuelson claims is the "most famous African American restaurant in the country."[142]

---

139 Tasty. 2016. *Fried Chicken As Made By Marcus Samuelsson*. Video.
140 Ibid.
141 "About". 2018. *Red Rooster Harlem*. Accessed October 14. http://www.redroosterharlem.com/aboutus/#the-people.
142 Tasty. 2016. *Fried Chicken As Made By Marcus Samuelsson*. Video.

Tasty, Food Republic, and any other food media platform lend a microphone and spotlight to these cuisines. It is a new point of entry for Ethiopian food into fine dining and an ode to what culinary traditions Samuelsson and Chapman nod to with Red Rooster.

When Recode asked Samuelsson if the "explosion" of food media changed the way he and other professional chefs cook and present food, and if diners' expectations have also responded, he paused to think for a moment. His answer boiled down to three main topics:

- Access: No longer must a chef rise into the culinary world through French cuisine or a diner know only regional flavors. The online space opens up endless points of access into food dialogue.
- Connection: According to Samuelsson, the significance of individuality and narrative has reached a new high. People crave distinction, and sit down to a meal to discover singluar perspective
- Engagement: Flavors have become a response to curiosity, a means of knowing and relating to others. Recipes, photos, stories and reviews beg for interaction with a world greater than a screen in your hand.

In Samuelsson's *Tasty* video, these points are all apparent.

I, in my cramped apartment, can make fried chicken like Marcus Samuelsson guided by a two-minute video. I want to try Red Rooster's "Fried Yard Bird" because I know the berbere in the chicken shake has a meaning sourced from personal story. And, when next in New York, I will make my way to Harlem to try it for myself. Access, connection, and engagement – the Food Internet in whole.

ACKNOWLEDGMENTS

———

This book would not have been possible without the knowledge and kindness of my interviewees. Our conversations served as both the backbone to this text and my fuel throughout the research, writing, editing and publishing process. I cannot thank you all enough.

To my friends and family, I owe you even more. Thank you for tolerating innumerable conversations about this single topic, for cheering me on, and bringing me to know the joy of a meal with loved ones. In particular, thank you to Skyler and Henry who assumed the roles of ruthless editors and remained by my side throughout.

Finally, thank you to New Degree Press, namely Eric Koester, Brian Bies, and Anastasia Armendariz. In under a year, you have provided me the tools and guidance necessary to write this book and change the course of my education, career and life. Thank you.

APPENDIX

**PART I: A KID WITH AN ANDRIOD
AND A TREACHEROUS SPACE**

Gold, Jonathan. 2009. "A Year In Food: Changing Tastes". *Los Angeles Times*, , 2009. http://articles.latimes.com/2009/dec/27/opinion/la-oe-gold27-2009dec27.

Serious Eats. 2018. "Phil Rosenthal Is Anthony Bourdain Except Afraid Of Everything". Podcast. *Serious Eats*. https://www.seriouseats.com/2018/02/special-sauce-phil-rosenthal-is-anthony-bourdain-except-afraid-of-everything.html.

CHAPTER 1. CROISSANTS, COMPUTERS, AND COMMUTERS

Beaudry, Rachel. 2018. Rachel Beaudry—Eating the Internet Interview Anabelle Nuelle Interview by. In person. Phone.

Biasco, Paul. 2018. "La Fournette Chef Pierre Zimmermann To Open Lincoln Park Location". *Dnainfo Chicago*. https://www.dnainfo.com/chicago/20130806/lincoln-park/la-fournette-chef-pierre-zimmermann-open-lincoln-park-location/.

"Cafe Fleurette - Winnetka, IL". 2016. *Yelp*. https://www.yelp.com/biz/cafe-fleurette-winnetka?osq=cafe+fluerette.

Chang, Chi-an. 2018. "Café Fleurette's Croissant Is A Must Try". *Patch.Com*. https://patch.com/illinois/winnetka/caf-fleurette-s-croissant-is-a-must-try.

Décret No. 93-1074 Du 13 Septembre 1993. 1993. Vol. 2. Paris, France: Official Journal of the French Republic.

Elliott, Libby. 2018. "Small Space, Big Taste In Winnetka Train Station". *Daily North Shore*, , 2018. https://jwcdaily.com/2018/03/04/small-space-big-taste-in-winnetka-train-station/.

Kim, Woo Gon, Jun (Justin) Li, and Robert A. Brymer. 2016. "The Impact Of Social Media Reviews On Restaurant Performance: The Moderating Role Of Excellence Certificate". *International*

Journal Of Hospitality Management 55: 41-51. doi:10.1016/j. ijhm.2016.03.001.

"La Fournette - French Bakery". 2018. *Lafournette.Com*. Accessed October 12. https://lafournette.com/.

Lombard, Eilis. 2013. "Café Fleurette". *Spoon University*. https:// spoonuniversity.com/place/cafe-fleurette.

Lutz, Ashley. 2013. "Restaurant Manager Says Yelp Is Killing His Business". *Business Insider*. https://www.businessinsider.com/ owner-yelp-is-bad-for-small-business-2013-4.

Maginity, Megan. 2016. "Tucked-Away Café Fleurette Named 'Best Local Secret'". *The Winnetka Current*, , 2016. https://www. winnetkacurrent.com/dining-out/tucked-away-caf%C3%A9-fleurette-named-%E2%80%98best-local-secret%E2%80%99.

Moses, Lucia. 2018. "'We're In The Middle Of A Reckoning': At Digital Media Gathering, New Reality Sets In - Digiday". *Digiday*. https://digiday.com/marketing/reality-sets-in-at-ad-execs-annual-meeting/.

CHAPTER 2. UNCERTAIN TERRAIN

"Cooking Panda". 2018. *Cookingpanda.Com*. https://www.cookingpanda.com/.

Cooking Panda. 2018. *Cheddar Bacon Chicken Ranch Pasta*. Video. https://www.facebook.com/MrCookingPanda/videos/1900372163320800/.

Cooking Panda. 2018. *Fried Ice Cream*. Video. https://www.facebook.com/MrCookingPanda/videos/1873363382688345/.

Cooking Panda. 2018. *Jalapeño Popper Stuffed Bacon Chicken*. Video. https://www.facebook.com/MrCookingPanda/videos/1790536324304385/.

Moses, Lucia. 2018. "Onetime Social Publishing Star Cooking Panda Is Shutting Down - Digiday". *Digiday*. https://digiday.com/media/onetime-social-publishing-star-cooking-panda-shutting/.

Moses, Lucia. 2018. "'We're In The Middle Of A Reckoning': At Digital Media Gathering, New Reality Sets In - Digiday". *Digiday*. https://digiday.com/marketing/reality-sets-in-at-ad-execs-annual-meeting/.

Mullin, Benjamin. 2018. "Cooking Panda Owner Is The Latest Digital Publisher To Shut Down After Facebook Changes". *WSJ*. https://www.wsj.com/articles/cooking-panda-owner-is-the-latest-digital-publisher-to-shut-down-after-facebook-changes-1522277679.

"Render Media Honored In The Top 2% Of The 2016 Inc. 5000 List". 2018. *Prnewswire.Com*. https://www.prnewswire.com/news-releases/render-media-honored-in-the-top-2-of-the-2016-inc-5000-list-300316076.html.

Sangal, Aditi. 2018. "Buzzfeed'S Jonah Peretti: 'We'Ve Proven We Can Be Profitable'". Podcast. *Digiday Podcast*. https://digiday.com/podcast/digiday-podcast-jonah-peretti-buzzfeed-facebook/.

Willens, Max. 2018. Max Willens—Eating the Internet Anabelle Nuelle Interview by . In person. Phone.

Willens, Max. 2018. "Facebook's New Branded-Content Guidelines Will Force Some Publishers To Abandon A Business Model - Digiday". *Digiday*. https://digiday.com/media/facebooks-new-branded-content-guidelines-will-force-publishers-abandon-business-model/.

PART II: ACCESS

Bourdain, Anthony. 2010. *Medium Raw: A Bloody Valentine To The World Of Food And The People Who Cook*. 1st ed. New York: HarperCollins Publishers.

Chang, David. 2018. "David Chang's Kitchen: My Name Is David Chang, And I Hate Fancy Beer". *GQ*. https://www.gq.com/story/david-chang-cheap-beer.

Fuhrmeister, Chris. 2018. "'Chef's Table: Pastry' Recap: Christina Tosi Channeled Her Childlike Wonder Into A Dessert Empire". *Eater*. https://www.eater.com/2018/4/13/17230656/chefs-table-pastry-christina-tosi-recap-episode-1.

Gold, Jonathan. 2018. "Anthony Bourdain opened the working-class kitchen to the world and the world to us". *Latimes. Com*. http://www.latimes.com/food/jonathan-gold/la-fo-gold-anthony-bourdain-20180608-story.html.

Roberts, Daniel. 2018. "David Chang Broke All The Rules | TIME. Com". *TIME.Com*. http://business.time.com/2013/09/26/david-chang-broke-all-the-rules/.

Smith, Aaron, and Monica Anderson. 2018. "Social Media Use 2018". Pew Research Center. http://www.pewinternet.org/2018/03/01/social-media-use-in-2018/.

Tandoh, Ruby. 2018. "Click Plate: How Instagram Is Changing The Way We Eat". *The Guardian*. https://www.theguardian.com/lifeandstyle/2016/nov/02/click-plate-how-instagram-changing-way-we-eat-food.

CHAPTER 3. EVERYONE'S A FOODIE

2017. Blog. *@Bitches_Quest_4_Queso*. https://www.instagram.com/
bitches_quest_4_queso/.

"45 Go-To Pasta Recipes For Dinner Tonight". 2017. *Country Living*.
https://www.countryliving.com/food-drinks/g1487/pasta-rec-
ipes/.

"Admissions & Aid". 2018. *Georgetown.Edu*. Accessed October 13.
https://www.georgetown.edu/admissions.

Burd, Sara. 2017. "The 4 Best Bagel Sandwiches In Charleston".
Spoon University. https://spoonuniversity.com/lifestyle/the-
4-bagel-sandwiches-in-charleston-ranked.

Celenza, Frankie. 2018. "Italian-American Food Never Claimed
To Be Italian, So You Can Stop Hating On It". *Huffpost.
Com/Life/*. https://www.huffpost.com/entry/italian-ameri-
can-food_n_5b364d53e4b08c3a8f69c37c.

Conley, Ellie. 2018. "Color Changing Gin Exists, And It Will
Make Your Gin & Tonic Turn Pink". *Spoon University*. https://
spoonuniversity.com/lifestyle/color-changing-gin-exists-and-
it-will-upgrade-your-gin-and-tonic.

De Laurentiis, Giada. 2018. "Chicken Tetrazzini | Recipes". *Food-
network.Com*. Accessed October 13. https://www.foodnetwork.

com/recipes/giada-de-laurentiis/chicken-tetrazzini-recipe-1943960.

Ferdman, Roberto A. 2016. "Stop Calling Yourself A 'Foodie'". *Washington Post*. https://www.washingtonpost.com/news/wonk/wp/2016/03/01/why-the-word-foodie-is-terrible-and-needs-to-go-away/?noredirect=on&utm_term=.e12c25950f6c.

"Find Your Campus". 2018. *Spoonuniversity.Com*. https://spoonuniversity.com/campuses.

Fuscaldo, Donna. 2017. "Instagram: 59% Of U.S. Millennials Are Active Users". *Investopedia*. https://www.investopedia.com/news/instagram-59-us-millennials-are-active-users/.

Hepner, Jen. 2018. "Bluestone Lane DC Has Arrived, And It's Amazingly Basic". *Spoon University*. https://spoonuniversity.com/place/bluestone-lane-dc-has-arrived-and-it-amazingly-basic.

Lanchester, John. 2014. "Shut Up And Eat". *The New Yorker*. https://www.newyorker.com/magazine/2014/11/03/shut-eat.

McCarthy, Niall. 2018. "Infographic: Half Of Americans Take Pictures Of Their Food". *Statista Infographics*. https://www.statista.com/chart/12776/half-of-americans-take-pictures-of-their-food/.

McCurry Hahn, Saoirse. 2017. "I Asked 9 People To Define The Term "Foodie" And Their Answers Were Surprisingly Different". *Spoon University*. https://spoonuniversity.com/lifestyle/9-people-offer-their-own-definitions-of-the-term-foodie.

Orr, Cassidy. 2018. "8 Back To School Breakfast Ideas For Busy College Students". *Spoon University*. https://spoonuniversity.com/lifestyle/8-back-to-school-breakfast-ideas-for-busy-college-students.

Paul, Eve. 2018. "How To Manage Millennials? Spoon University Cracked The Code And Is Reaping The Rewards". *Forbes*. https://www.forbes.com/sites/eveturowpaul/2016/11/21/how-to-manage-millennials-spoon-university-cracked-the-code-and-is-reaping-the-rewards/.

Peele, Anna. 2016. "Just How Food-Obsessed Is The Typical Millennial?". *Bon Appetit*. https://www.bonappetit.com/entertaining-style/pop-culture/article/millennials-and-food.

Spindler, Samantha. 2018. "The Mdining Changes You Need To Know About". *Spoon University*. https://spoonuniversity.com/healthier/mdining-is-listenting-to-the-students.

"Spoon University | The Food Resource For Our Generation". 2018. *Spoonuniversity.Com*. Accessed October 14. https://spoonuniversity.com/.

Tandoh, Ruby. 2016. "Click Plate: How Instagram Is Changing The Way We Eat". *The Guardian*. https://www.theguardian.com/lifeandstyle/2016/nov/02/click-plate-how-instagram-changing-way-we-eat-food.

te Wildt, Sydney. 2018. "Kylie Jenner's Top Pregnancy Craving Was Eggo Waffles". *Spoon University*. https://spoonuniversity.com/lifestyle/kylie-jenner-top-pregnancy-craving-was-eggo-waffles.

"The Food Resource For Our Generation". 2018. *Spoonuniversity.Com*. https://spoonuniversity.com/about.

CHAPTER 4. NEW CHANNELS

"61% Of Young Adults In U.S. Watch Mainly Streaming TV". 2018. *Pew Research Center*. http://www.pewresearch.org/fact-tank/2017/09/13/about-6-in-10-young-adults-in-u-s-primarily-use-online-streaming-to-watch-tv/.

"About YouTube". 2018. *Youtube.Com*. https://www.youtube.com/yt/about/.

Celenza, Frankie. 2018. "Frankie Celenza". *Tisch.Nyu.Edu*. https://tisch.nyu.edu/clive-davis-institute/alumni/frankiecelenza.

Celenza, Frankie. 2018. "Italian-American Food Never Claimed To Be Italian, So You Can Stop Hating On It". *Huffpost Life*. https://www.huffpost.com/entry/italian-american-food_n_5b-364d53e4b08c3a8f69c37c.

Celenza, Frankie. 2018. Preliminary "Eating the Internet" InterviewAnabelle Nuelle Interview by . In person. Phone.

CHAPTER 5. NEW VOICES AND FLAVORS

Carman, Tim. 2012. "New Young & Hungry Columnist Anonymous". *Washington Post*. https://www.washingtonpost.com/blogs/all-we-can-eat/post/new-young-and-hungry-columnist-wont-be-anonymous/2012/05/02/gIQArXaJxT_blog.html?utm_term=.f5c27f744e37&wprss=rss_all-we-can-eat.

Chopra, Sonia. 2018. Eating the Internet Interview Anabelle Nuelle Interview by . In person. Phone.

Krishna, Priya. 2018. "Why An Ancient Frozen Japanese Specialty Is America'S Hottest Dessert". *Grub Street*. http://www.grubstreet.com/2018/03/kakigori-pastry-chefs.html.

McKeever, Amy. 2018. "City Paper Editor Michael Schaffer On Critics & Anonymity". *Eater DC*. https://dc.eater.com/2012/5/3/6590261/city-paper-editor-michael-schaffer-on-critics-anonymity.

Rojas, Warren. 2018. "Isabella Eatery Manager Sues Mike Isabella For Sexual Harassment [Updated]". *Eater DC*. https://dc.eater. com/2018/3/19/17139870/mike-isabella-chloe-caras-sexual-harassment.

Severson, Kim. 2018. "James Beard Awards Apply A New Yardstick: Good Behavior". *Nytimes.Com*. https://www.nytimes. com/2018/02/15/dining/james-beard-awards-sexual-harassment.html.

Sidman, Jessica. 2018. "Eating the Internet" – Interview Anabelle Nuelle Interview by. In person. Phone.

Sidman, Jessica. 2015. "Investigation Reveals Fig & Olive's Kitchen Relies On Pre-Made Meal Components". *Washington City Paper*. https://www.washingtoncitypaper.com/food/ blog/20678796/investigation-finds-fig-olives-kitchen-relies-on-pre-made-meal-components.

Swift, Art. 2018. "Americans' Trust In Mass Media Sinks To New Low". *Gallup.Com*. https://news.gallup.com/poll/195542/americans-trust-mass-media-sinks-new-low.aspx.

The New York Times. 1859. "How We Dine", Anonymous, 1859. https://timesmachine.nytimes.com/timesmachine/1859/01/01/78882285.pdf.

Vo, Lam Thuy. 2017. "We Got Government Data On 20 Years Of Workplace Sexual Harassment Claims. These Charts Break It Down.". *Buzzfeednews.Com*. https://www.buzzfeednews.com/article/lamvo/eeoc-sexual-harassment-data#.svGEBJPrVV.

PART III: CONNECT

Serious Eats. 2018. "Phil Rosenthal Is Anthony Bourdain Except Afraid Of Everything". Podcast. *Serious Eats*. https://www.seriouseats.com/2018/02/special-sauce-phil-rosenthal-is-anthony-bourdain-except-afraid-of-everything.html.

Walker, Christina, and Saeed Ahmed. 2018. "There Has Been, On Average, 1 School Shooting Every Week This Year". *CNN*. https://www.cnn.com/2018/03/02/us/school-shootings-2018-list-trnd/index.html.

"Why Stress Causes People To Overeat - Harvard Health". 2018. *Harvard Health*. https://www.health.harvard.edu/newsletter_article/why-stress-causes-people-to-overeat.

CHAPTER 6. MAKING IT PERSONAL

"Bon Appétit Magazine: Recipes, Cooking, Entertaining, Restaurants". 2018. *Bonappetit.Com*. https://www.bonappetit.com/.

"Epicurious – Recipes, Menu Ideas, Videos & Cooking Tips". 2018. *Epicurious.Com*. https://www.epicurious.com/.

Food Innovation Group. 2018. "Home - Food Innovation Group". *Foodinnovationgroup.Com*. http://www.foodinnovationgroup. com/.

Main, Sami. 2018. "Food52 And The Unique Space It Occupies On The Food Internet". *Adweek.Com*. https://www.adweek. com/digital/food52-and-the-unique-space-it-occupies-on-the-food-internet/.

Main, Sami. 2018. "How Condé Nast's Food Innovation Group Plans To Take Over The 'Food Internet'". *Adweek.Com*. https:// www.adweek.com/digital/how-cond-nasts-food-innovation-group-plans-take-over-food-internet-175101/.

Main, Sami. 2018. "Why Genius Kitchen Serves Up Relatable Food Content To Millennials". *Adweek.Com*. https://www.adweek. com/creativity/why-genius-kitchen-serves-up-relatable-food-content-to-millennials/.

NPR. 2017. "Why Eating The Same Food Increases People's Trust And Cooperation". Podcast. *Morning Edition*. https://www.npr. org/2017/02/02/512998465/why-eating-the-same-food-increases-peoples-trust-and-cooperation.

Shearer, Elisa, and Jeffrey Gottfried. 2018. "News Use Across Social Media Platforms 2017". *Pew Research Center's Journalism Project*. http://www.journalism.org/2017/09/07/news-use-across-social-media-platforms-2017/.

Sifton, Sam. Letter Anabelle Nuelle to. 2018. "Cooking: What I Did On My Summer Vacation". Email, 2018.

Sifton, Sam. 2018. Interview 1 - Eating the Internet Anabelle Nuelle Interview by. In person. Phone.

Sifton, Sam. 2010. "Kenmare". *The New York Times | Food*, , 2010. https://www.nytimes.com/2010/07/07/dining/reviews/07rest.html?ref=samsifton.

CHAPTER 7. "INSTAGRAM, A COMMUNITY OF OVER 1 BILLION..."

2018. Blog. *@Popeyethefoodie*. https://www.instagram.com/p/Bd6cvEEHqbO/?taken-by=popeyethefoodie.

Chau, Mike. 2018. Blog. *@Foodbabyny*. Accessed July 13. https://www.instagram.com/foodbabyny/.

Chen, Yuyu. 2017. "What Influencer Marketing Really Costs". *Digiday*. https://digiday.com/marketing/what-influencer-marketing-costs/.

Cooke, Jayna. 2018. "Is It Worth Sharing? Corbett Drummey And The Question That Built Popular Pays". *Forbes*. https://www.forbes.com/sites/jaynacooke/2018/01/12/is-it-worth-sharing-corbett-drummey-and-the-question-that-built-popular-pays/#5c1108d5356f.

Dunbar, R. I. M. 2017. "Breaking Bread: The Functions Of Social Eating". *Adaptive Human Behavior And Physiology* 3 (3): 198-211. doi:10.1007/s40750-017-0061-4.

Ferguson, Gillian. 2017. "How Los Angeles Became One of the Best Food Cities in the World". *Food & Wine*. https://www.foodandwine.com/travel/restaurants/best-food-cities-2017-los-angeles.

Iida, Tucker. 2018. Tucker Iida - Eating the Internet Anabelle Nuelle Interview by . In person. Phone.

"Influencer". 2018. *Cambridge Dictionary*. Cambridge University Press. https://dictionary.cambridge.org/us/dictionary/english/influencer.

"About Us • Instagram". 2018. *Instagram.Com*. https://www.instagram.com/about/us/.

Kramer, Jillian. 2018. "How to Become a Food Instagram Influencer". *Food & Wine*. https://www.foodandwine.com/how-to-be-food-influencer.

Larocca, Amy. 2018. "How Influencers Became The New Fashion Establishment". *The Cut*. https://www.thecut.com/2018/02/instagram-influencers-are-the-new-fashion-establishment.html.

"Popular Pays: Create Content Worth Sharing". 2018. *Popular Pays*. https://www.popularpays.com/.

"Takasan". 2018. *Takasan.*. Accessed October 13. https://www.takasan.co/.

"Takasan: Bowling For Your Buds". 2017. *LA Downtowner*. https://www.ladowntowner.com/articles/2018/2/takasan.

"The 15 Hottest Los Angeles Cheap Eats Restaurants". 2018. *Eater LA*. https://la.eater.com/maps/best-los-angeles-cheap-eats-affordable-restaurants.

CHAPTER 8. CONNECTION OFFLINE

Butler, Sharon. 2017. "A Brief History Of Food As Art". *Smithsonian*. https://www.smithsonianmag.com/travel/food-art-cultural-travel-180961648/.

Ebner, Tim. 2018. "12 Essential D.C. Steakhouses To Try". *Eater DC*. https://dc.eater.com/maps/best-steakhouses-dc-washington-meat.

Ebner, Tim. 2018. Tim Ebner—Eating the Internet Anabelle Nuelle Interview by . In person.

Hobson, Katherine. 2017. "Feeling Lonely? Too Much Time on Social Media May Be Why". *Npr.Org*. https://www.npr.org/sections/health-shots/2017/03/06/518362255/feeling-lonely-too-much-time-on-social-media-may-be-why.

Kim, Sam. 2018. "Where To Eat In And Around NYC'S Koreatown". *Eater NY*. https://ny.eater.com/maps/best-koreatown-restaurants-nyc.

Lin, Helen Lee. 2012. "How Your Cell Phone Hurts Your Relationships". *Scientific American*. https://www.scientificamerican.com/article/how-your-cell-phone-hurts-your-relationships/.

Primack, Brian A., Ariel Shensa, Jaime E. Sidani, Erin O. Whaite, Liu yi Lin, Daniel Rosen, Jason B. Colditz, Ana Radovic, and Elizabeth Miller. 2017. "Social Media Use And Perceived Social Isolation Among Young Adults In The U.S.". *American Journal Of Preventive Medicine* 53 (1): 1-8. doi:10.1016/j.amepre.2017.01.010.

Sevigny, Mellissa. 2018. "Easy Lemon Cheesecake - Low Carb & Keto | I Breathe I'm Hungry". *I Breathe I'm Hungry*. Accessed October 13. https://www.ibreatheimhungry.com/easy-lemon-cheesecake-low-carb-keto/.

Turkle, Sherry. 2012. *Connected, But Alone?*. Video. https://www.ted.com/talks/sherry_turkle_alone_together.

Whitten, Sarah. 2018. "6 Foods You Will Be Eating In 2018". *CNBC*. https://www.cnbc.com/2017/12/27/6-foods-you-will-be-eating-in-2018.html.

Willingham, AJ. 2017. "Study Links Social Media Use To Isolation In Young Adults". *CNN*. https://www.cnn.com/2017/03/06/health/social-media-isolation-study-trnd/index.html.

Wood, Kate. 2018. "Apple Crisp Ice Cream". *Wood & Spoon*. http://thewoodandspoon.com/apple-crisp-ice-cream/.

Wood, Kate. 2018. Kate Wood—Eating the Internet Interview Anabelle Interview by . In person. Phone.

CHAPTER 9. THE OLD IS NEW AGAIN

Butler, Sharon. 2017. "A Brief History Of Food As Art". *Smithsonian Magazine*. https://www.smithsonianmag.com/travel/food-art-cultural-travel-180961648/.

Cézanne, Paul. 1905. *Still Life With Apples And Peaches*. Oil on canvas. Washington, D.C.: The National Gallery.

Ellner, David. 2018. David Ellner—Eating the Internet InterviewAnabelle Nuelle Interview by . In person. Phone.

Jackson, Drew. 2018. "James Beard Award Given To Vivian Howard-Hosted Video. Next Up, The Daytime Emmys.". *Newsobserver*. https://www.newsobserver.com/living/article210047779.html.

Martin, Adam. 2012. "Meet The Father Of Modern Restaurant Criticism". *The Atlantic*. https://www.theatlantic.com/entertainment/archive/2012/05/meet-father-modern-restaurant-criticism/328406/.

Meléndez, Luiz. 1772. *Still Life With Salmon, Lemon And Three Vessels*. Oil on canvas. Madrid, Spain: Museo Del Prado.

Meléndez, Luiz. 1772. *The Afternoon Meal (La Merienda)*. Oil on canvas. New York, New York: The Metropolitan Museum of Art.

Panna Cooking. 2018. *Black Bean-Glazed Salmon With Cabbage By Vivian Howard*. Video. Accessed October 14. https://www.pannacooking.com/recipes/black-bean-glazed-salmon-ginger-cabbage-vivian-howard/.

Relief: Two Servants Bearing Food And Drink. n.d. Limestone. New York, New York: The Metropolitan Museum of Art.

Sévigné, Marie de Rabutin-Chantal, and Leonard Tancock. 1982. *Selected Letters Of Madame De Sevigne ; Translated With An Introduction By Leonard Tancock*. Harmondsworth: Penguin.

Sifton, Sam. 2018. Sam Sifton—Eating the Internet Interviews 1&2 Anabelle Nuelle Interview by . In person. Phone.

"The New York Times Cook Book". 2018. *Amazon.Com*. Accessed October 14. https://www.amazon.com/New-York-Times-Cook-Book/dp/0060160101.

Wilbur, Kenzi. 2013. "David Ellner, Founder Of The Panna Cooking App (And A Giveaway!)". *Food52*. https://food52.com/blog/5423-david-ellner-founder-of-the-panna-cooking-app-and-a-giveaway.

CHAPTER 10. THE TRUST TEST

Brown, Pat. 2018. "What IF?". Blog. *Medium*. https://medium.com/impossible-foods/the-mission-that-motivates-us-d4d7de61665.

Chaey, Christina. 2016. "The Fake-Meat Burger So Realistic It Fooled My Entire Family". *Bon Appetit*. https://www.bonappetit.com/entertaining-style/trends-news/article/impossible-burger-fake-meat.

Cotcamp, Lexi. 2018. Lexi Cotcamp—Eating the InternetAnabelle Nuelle Interview by . In person. Phone.

Main, Sami. 2018. Sami Main—Eating the Internet Interview Anabelle Nuelle Interview by. In person. Phone.

McSpadden, Kevin. 2015. "You Now Have a Shorter Attention Span Than a Goldfish". *Time*. http://time.com/3858309/attention-spans-goldfish/.

"Mission | Impossible Foods". 2018. *Impossible Foods*. Accessed October 14. https://impossiblefoods.com/mission.

Pat Brown, Impossible Foods. 2018. "Open Letter From The CEO". Accessed October 15. https://www.impossiblefoods.com/letter-from-the-ceo/.

"Pat Brown". 2018. *TEDMED*. https://www.tedmed.com/speakers/show?id=526389.

Polis, Carey. 2018. Carey Polis—Eating the Internet Interview Anabelle Nuelle Interview by . In person. Phone.

CHAPTER 11. THE ENGAGEMENT EMPIRE

"About". 2018. *WPP Stream*. Accessed October 14. http://wppstream. com/events/stream-usa-2017/about/.

"About". 2018. *Red Rooster Harlem*. Accessed October 14. http:// www.redroosterharlem.com/aboutus/#the-people.

Code Media. 2017. *Full Video: Tasty GM Ashley Mccollum And Chef Marcus Samuelsson At Code Media*. Video. https://www. recode.net/2017/3/18/14958934/video-watch-food-buzzfeed-tasty-gm-ashley-mccollum-chef-marcus-samuelsson-code-media.

Former Tasty Employee Interview. 2018 Anabelle Nuelle Interview by . In person. Phone.

Hustle Co. 2018. *Ashley Mccollum | GM Of Tasty @ Buzzfeed*. Video. https://www.youtube.com/watch?v=y7RcwQ4ni10.

"Marcus Samuelsson Bio". 2018. *Foodnetwork.Com*. https://www. foodnetwork.com/profiles/talent/marcus-samuelsson/bio.

McCollum, Ashley. 2016. 5 MIN TALK: Making Sharable Content with Ashley McCollum, General Manager, Tasty, Buzzfeed Jonathan Cloonan Interview by . In person. Stream USA 2016.

Peterson, Jason. 2018. Jason Peterson—Eating the Internet Anabelle Nuelle Interview by . In person. Phone.

Romm, Cari. 2015. "What 'Food Porn' Does To The Brain". *The Atlantic*. https://www.theatlantic.com/health/archive/2015/04/what-food-porn-does-to-the-brain/390849/.

Tasty. 2016. *Fried Chicken As Made By Marcus Samuelsson*. Video. https://www.youtube.com/watch?v=k7MafUNvuXs.

Tasty. 2018. *Sliders 4 Ways*. Video. Accessed October 14. https://www.tasty.co/compilation/sliders-4-ways#4ldradw.

Willens, Max. 2018. Max Willens—Eating the Internet Anabelle Nuelle Interview by . In person. Phone.

Willens, Max. 2017. "Signs That Facebook Food Videos Are Losing Their Luster - Digiday". *Digiday*. https://digiday.com/media/signs-facebook-food-videos-losing-luster/.

Made in the USA
Middletown, DE
25 June 2020